Making & Baking
Gingerbread
Houses

Making & Baking
Gingerbread Houses

WRITTEN AND ILLUSTRATED BY

Lauren Jarrett
& Nancy Nagle

CROWN PUBLISHERS, INC. NEW YORK

Dedicated to the long line
of family, friends and mentors
from whom one learns
to cook, look, live and love.

ACKNOWLEDGMENTS

With appreciation to Joe Freedman and Laura Ross of Cognoscenti Books, who came up with the idea and helped to see it through; special thanks to Pam Thomas for all her support; and Jim Davis of Crown Publishers for his time and help. Thanks also to Ann Hasselberger for loaning us cake decorators; Susan Bennett, our audience and overseer; and to Willie and Eric for encouraging us and liking cookies.

Inquiries should be addressed to Crown Publishers, Inc., One Park Avenue, New York, New York 10016

Printed in the United States of America

Published simultaneously in Canada by General Publishing Company Limited

Library of Congress Cataloging in Publication Data
Jarrett, Lauren.
Making & baking gingerbread houses.

1. Gingerbread. 2. Gingerbread houses.
I. Nagle, Nancy. II. Title. III. Title: Making and baking gingerbread houses.
TX771.J39 1984 641.8'65 84-20071
ISBN 0-517-55598-0 (pbk.)

Produced by Cognoscenti Books

Word Processing: Scribes, Inc.

Typesetting: Maxwell Photographics, Inc.

ISBN: 0-517-55598-0

10 9 8 7 6 5 4 3 2 1

First edition

CONTENTS

1

•••••••••••••••••

HISTORY OF
GINGERBREAD

*"Had I but one penny in the world,
thou shouldst have it for gingerbread."*
—William Shakespeare
Love's Labour's Lost

Your first experience with gingerbread probably came as a child listening to the Grimm brothers' tale of Hansel, Gretel, and the witch. But in fact, the tradition of making treats with this pungent spice dates back through many centuries and across several continents. It is quite a story in itself.

Ginger was a plant native to China and India—where much of the world's supply is still grown. Arab traders introduced it to the Greeks. Like the Chinese, the Greeks appreciated ginger's medicinal properties such as aiding digestion, preventing colds, and restoring appetites. The ancient Romans used ginger as a remedy for the plague and enjoyed its spicy flavor for cooking. Returning Crusaders brought back ginger along with other treasures from the East.

The English fashioned medicinal ginger candies called "gingerbrati" in the 13th century. During the next century gingerbrati changed as breadcrumbs were added to the candy and it became known as "gingerbrede."

It was the 14th-century Germans who really began to take gingerbread seriously, so seriously, in fact, that they formed special guilds of gingerbread artisans, distinct from the existing baking guilds. With their specialized skills, they created fanciful and elaborate depictions of aristocratic life. These creations were stamped from carved molds, decorated with real leaves, painted with gold leaf, and studded with cloves dipped in gold leaf. When complete they sometimes weighed as much as 150 pounds! The Germans may have been the first Europeans to fashion shapes and figures from gingerbread, but Queen Elizabeth I of England is credited with first presenting gingerbread likenesses to her guests.

In the early 17th century, the French and English added eggs, flour, and honey to the recipe. At about this time, the English also began adding molasses, a sugar derivative, available from the New World colonies. Later in the century, gingerbread creations were made for the bourgeois as well as aristocratic patron to celebrate all manner of holidays.

In the next century, peasant themes and animal shapes became popular. This is probably when the first gingerbread cottages were built. The Grimm brothers had written their tale about Hansel and Gretel, which described a house "made of bread, with a roof of cake and windows of barley." The gingerbread house was born, and has been with us ever since.

Throughout the 19th century, finely crafted gingerbread was used to express greetings, recognition, affection, and celebration. The heart-shaped gingerbread valentine was especially popular. As the gingerbread shapes became more commercial, many details and ornamentations were simplified, but the holiday custom of making gingerbread is still popular throughout Europe. Large, elaborate figures are made in Belgium and Holland to usher in St. Nicholas Day. Scandinavian children know Christmas is coming when they spy some pig-shaped gingerbread cookies in the bakery window.

In the United States, gingerbread has been popular since Colonial days. Salem, Massachusetts was an important spice trading center, so ginger flavored concoctions were—and still are—specialties of the New England area. Ginger even played a role in our history: George Washington's mother was famous for her spicy gingerbread, and ginger was included in the rations of Revolutionary soldiers, both for its medicinal value, and to add flavor to otherwise simple and sparse meals.

Before the Civil War, a holiday evolved on the first Tuesday in June, known as Muster Day. Spectators turned out to watch the town's militia parade. Muster Day became a New England tradition—changing later from a militia spectacle to a day of competitions among firefighting teams. Gingerbread cookies were an integral part of this celebration, and continue to be the traditional treat of this day, now reserved for family picnics.

A tradition as long-standing as the baking of gingerbread yields great rewards. Besides filling your house with its wonderful aroma as it bakes, and satisfying the appetites of family and friends with its spicy sweetness, a gingerbread project makes an afternoon pass with utter delight. The gingerbread houses in this book span a broad range of architectural styles from the simple Hansel & Gretel cottage to the elaborate Victorian mansion. Before choosing one special project to build, be sure to read the "Gingerbread Basics," page 9. This chapter will provide all the guidance you'll need to build your gingerbread house. Remember to make plenty of cookies from the chapter called "More Cookies" page 123 to populate the house; they're the first thing to be eaten, and having plenty is the best insurance for your house's survival. Alone or with the family, for party decor or as a gift, enjoy your gingerbread structure and become a part of a folk tradition stretching back through the centuries.

2

·•·•·•·•·•·•·•·•·•·•·•·•·

GINGERBREAD BASICS

A gingerbread house just may be the perfect family project: fun and creative to make, impressive to look at—and delicious. Whether you start with a classic Hansel & Gretel cottage or a Victorian mansion, you'll find the afternoon flies by—even for the most restless young helper—and the result will be a sense of pride and accomplishment that's hard to match. Your decorated gingerbread house will certainly produce exclamations of amazement from friends and party guests.

What better way to celebrate Halloween than with a spooky, haunted gingerbread house? Or, how about an ice cream and candy-laden gingerbread train for your child's next birthday party? The possibilities are endless.

All the houses in the following chapters use the basic construction techniques described in this chapter. Read this one first before picking out one special house to build. Follow the plans as closely as possible, especially when you are starting out.

If you work straight through, the entire construction process will take about five hours. (The pattern pieces can be prepared in advance if you wish—an especially good idea if you have impatient helpers.)

Basically, you need to follow these eight steps:

1. Collect ingredients and equipment

2. Prepare pattern pieces

3. Clear kitchen table and counters

4. Mix and roll out dough

5. Cut pieces—bake and trim

6. Mix icing and glaze

7. Assemble pieces step by step

8. Decorate and enjoy

COLLECTING INGREDIENTS & EQUIPMENT

Most of the equipment you need can be found right in your kitchen. Assembling it ahead of time saves you from last-minute searching:

2 or 3 large mixing bowls	Spatula
Rolling pin	Cookie cutters (use them
Measuring cups and spoons	to make extra cookies)
2 or 3 cookie sheets	Serving tray for a base
Parchment paper for cooling	Pastry bag with tips or a cake
Wooden spoons	decorator with tips
Small paring knife for	Brush for glaze
trimming	Candy and nuts for decorations

You'll also need a few common household supplies that might be found in other rooms in the house:

Wooden ruler	String
Scissors	Pencils

In addition, you'll need *heavy-weight tracing vellum*, described later in the pattern section, for making patterns.

PREPARING THE PATTERN PIECES

All the pattern pieces in this book are full scale and ready to use. Some large pattern pieces have been folded (fold lines are dotted).

To begin, obtain a pad of 11" x 14" heavy-weight tracing vellum from an art supply store or good stationery store. (Avoid light-weight tracing paper as it won't hold up to the moist dough.) Place a piece of the vellum over each pattern piece. Use the pencil and ruler to trace the outline of the patterns. Be sure to trace all the window and door openings, and label each pattern piece with its name and the number of gingerbread pieces you need to make from it. It is helpful to label the pattern pieces, especially in cases where you need both a right and left version of the same piece. Using a scissors, cut out the basic pieces, then cut out the windows and doors.

To cut out a folded pattern piece, fold a sheet of tracing vellum in half. Place the fold on the dotted line of the pattern piece. Trace the pattern outline and the door and window openings. Keep the vellum folded. Cut out the pattern piece and the door and window openings. Unfold the vellum and you have a full pattern.

The heavy-weight tracing vellum will last through several cuttings and trimmings, but for patterns that you will use more often—such as trees, animals and people—you should make a more durable pattern. Cut out the pattern on vellum, as described above. Then place the vellum pattern on a piece of construction paper or light cardboard. Make a pencil outline around the shape and cut it out. The construction paper or light cardboard pattern will be sturdier when you want to make lots of cookies.

Cutting Right and Left Pieces

A note on each pattern piece will tell you how many gingerbread pieces you'll need to make. (If there is nothing marked, you'll need only one.) On some pattern pieces, the words "cut a right and a left" will appear. (The baked pieces have a rough side and a smooth side.) When tracing the pieces onto the vellum, always write down, right on the vellum, all the instructions written on the pattern piece, including the "cut a right and left" instruction.

When you're ready to cut the pattern piece out of gingerbread, check it for notes, and if it says "cut a right and left," you'll cut at least two pieces. Place the pattern on the dough with the writing face-up and cut around it. Then flip it so the writing is face-down and cut around it again. Later, you'll find you have all the parts you need.

CLEARING A SPACE

Building a gingerbread house takes a bit of space. Before starting, you might want to do some site preparation by clearing a space to work. You'll need room to mix and roll out the dough; another place for the pieces to cool while you're making more house parts or cookies (2 or 3 feet of space at least), and finally, you'll need ample room at table height to assemble and decorate the house.

Align the folded edge of the vellum with the dotted line of the pattern piece

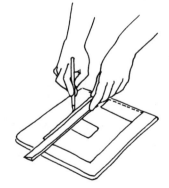

Trace the outline of the pattern and cut it out

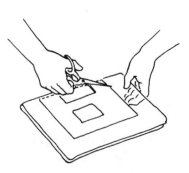

MIXING THE DOUGH

Here is the basic gingerbread dough with directions for mixing it.

BASIC GINGERBREAD DOUGH

1 cup melted butter (salted)	2 tablespoons hot coffee
1½ cups dark brown sugar	4 teaspoons cinnamon
1 egg	3 teaspoons ginger
2 tablespoons molasses	3 teaspoons cloves
1 tablespoon dark corn syrup	2 teaspoons nutmeg
2 teaspoons baking soda	4 cups flour

Melt the butter in a small pan, keeping the burner or flame on low to prevent it from burning. Set the pan aside when the butter is melted.

Pack the brown sugar into the measuring cup with a spoon and empty it into a large bowl. Add the melted butter and cream the two together with a wooden spoon. Add 1 egg. Add the molasses and corn syrup.

In a measuring cup, mix the baking soda in the hot coffee and add to the large bowl.

Add the cinnamon, ginger, cloves, and nutmeg. Mix thoroughly by hand or with an electric mixer on medium speed.

Add the flour one cup at a time. Mix well with a wooden spoon. The dough should be quite stiff. Then use your hands to work the bits of dough together. Add up to ½ cup additional flour a bit at a time, if necessary.

Make 3 or 4 balls of the dough. Put them in a sealed plastic bag and chill them briefly (about 15 minutes) in the refrigerator.

Instructions for some of the houses in this book suggest using other varieties of gingerbread for some parts of the house or landscape. These variations provide a change of taste and color. All the recipes work perfectly well for all the houses or cookies, so feel free to substitute them wherever you wish.

Pack the brown sugar into a measuring cup with a spoon and empty it into a large bowl

Add the flour one cup at a time while mixing with a wooden spoon

CHOCOLATE COOKIE DOUGH

1 cup melted butter	2 tablespoons honey
4 squares unsweetened chocolate (4 oz.)	2 teaspoons baking soda
1½ cups dark brown sugar	2 tablespoons hot coffee
1 egg	1 tablespoon instant coffee (dry)
1 tablespoon dark corn syrup	4 cups flour

Melt the butter in a small pan, keeping the burner or flame on low to prevent it from burning. As you melt the butter, add the chocolate and blend while melting. Set the pan aside when the butter-chocolate mixture is melted.

Measure the brown sugar by packing it into the measuring cup with a spoon and empty it into a large bowl. Add the melted butter and chocolate mixture and cream together with a wooden spoon. Add 1 egg. Add the corn syrup and honey.

In a measuring cup mix the baking soda in the hot coffee and add to the large bowl. Mix all the ingredients well.

Add the instant coffee and the melted butter-chocolate mixture, mixing thoroughly by hand or with an electric mixer on medium speed.

Add the flour one cup at a time and mix well with a wooden spoon. The dough should be quite stiff. Then use your hands to work the bits of dough together. Add a bit more flour, if necessary.

Make 3 or 4 balls of the dough. Put them in a sealed plastic bag and chill them briefly (about 15 minutes) in the refrigerator.

VANILLA COOKIE DOUGH

1 cup melted butter	2 teaspoons baking soda
1½ cups light brown sugar	2 tablespoons hot coffee
1 egg	1 teaspoon vanilla extract
3 tablespoons maple syrup	4 cups flour

Melt the butter in a small pan, keeping the burner or flame on low to prevent it from burning. Set the pan aside when the butter is melted.

Measure the brown sugar by packing it into the measuring cup with a spoon and empty it into a large bowl. Add the melted butter and cream the two together with a wooden spoon. Add 1 egg. Add the maple syrup.

In a measuring cup mix the baking soda in the hot coffee and add to the large bowl. Mix all of the ingredients well.

Add the vanilla extract and the melted butter, mixing thoroughly by hand or with an electric mixer on medium speed.

Add the flour one cup at a time and mix well with a wooden spoon. The dough should be quite stiff. Then use your hands to work the bits of dough together. Sprinkle more flour if necessary.

Make 3 or 4 balls of the dough. Put them in a sealed plastic bag and chill them briefly (about 15 minutes) in the refrigerator.

ROLLING OUT THE DOUGH

Rolling out the dough on baking sheets is the easiest method and it cuts down on distortion and stretching of the house pieces. (One of the better cookie sheets is a double thickness variety available from Cushion-Aire.) Turn jelly roll pans or standard cookie sheets with sides upside down.

Grease the sheet with shortening, then flour lightly by sprinkling flour over the sheet and tapping it to remove the excess. When rolling the dough, lay a damp cloth *under* the baking sheet to keep it from slipping and sliding.

Preheat the oven to 350°.

Begin with a piece of the chilled dough. Form an oblong or rectangular shape with your hands and place it lengthwise on the cookie sheet. Flour the rolling pin and begin to roll out the dough, reflouring the rolling pin as you go along. Sprinkle the surface of the dough with flour if it seems too sticky. Roll the dough out to about 1/8" thickness, trying very hard to keep it an even thickness all around.

CUTTING THE PIECES

Place the paper pattern pieces on the dough, leaving 1/2" - 3/4" between the pieces. Fit them with care, so as to make the best use of your dough. If a pattern piece does not completely fit on the dough, cut an unused section and use it to fill out the area. Press it in place and roll the surface lightly until smooth. Replace the pattern piece on the dough and cut it out.

The tracing vellum will stick to the moist dough so you should not have any problem with the pattern paper shifting on the dough as you cut. Use the wooden ruler and paring knife to cut around the pieces. Cut out the doors and windows. The door and window pieces can be re-cut during baking and used on the finished house. Shutters are made by cutting down the middle of the window piece. Then use a spatula or paring knife to pick up

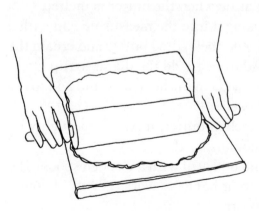

Roll out the dough to about 1/8" thickness on a greased baking sheet

If your pattern doesn't fit on the dough, fill out the corners with extra dough and roll smooth

Cut out the pieces using a ruler and paring knife

Carefully cut out the windows and doors and save them, if you want your house to have doors and shutters later

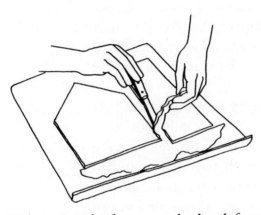

With a paring knife, remove the dough from around the pieces

Remove the paper pattern pieces and set them aside

the scrap dough around the pieces. The knife works well between the pieces and the spatula is good for the outside trimming.

Remove the paper pattern piece and set it aside for later use when trimming. Ball up scraps and return them to the plastic bag to add to the other dough.

BAKING AND TRIMMING

Bake the gingerbread at 350° for about 8 minutes, or until the dough is "half-baked." Then remove the sheet from the oven to see if the pieces need trimming. (They probably do.) Place it carefully on a board or hot pad and be very careful not to burn yourself. *This is definitely not a step to have your young assistants undertake.*

Place the pattern pieces over the half-baked dough. The pattern pieces will curl up from the heat, so hold them down with the wooden ruler. Check all the edges of the dough to see if they are straight, and trim any that extend over the outside of the pattern; straight sides are much easier to join together later on.

Return the gingerbread to the oven for another 4 minutes. The dough

Trim the edges of the half-baked cookies by checking them against the paper pattern pieces

will feel firm when it's done. Remove it from the oven and allow it to cool for a few minutes. Use a spatula to loosen the pieces—carefully—then transfer them to the sheets of parchment paper or flattened brown bags on a counter or table. Make sure the surface is flat—the cookies can still warp while they are warm. When thoroughly cooled, the pieces can be stacked if you are short on space.

Continue baking until you have all the necessary pieces. Be sure that you have made all the walls and other pieces you need, especially those that require using the same pattern several times. Use any extra dough to make people, animals, trees or other trimmings to go with your house and to snack on while you're working. You can roll out the dough for cookie shapes on the greased and floured cookie sheets and remove the excess, or you can roll the dough out on a board or table and lift the individual cookies with a spatula and transfer them to the greased cookie sheet. Remember that the best insurance for the safety of a gingerbread house is having enough cookies for everyone to snack on without attacking the house itself—until you're ready to serve it.

TAKING A BREAK

Gingerbread house-building does not need to be finished in one afternoon. If you prefer to spread the work out, the dough can be refrigerated for a few hours or a few days in a sealed plastic bag. Let it return to room temperature before you begin to roll it out.

Cooled cookies and house pieces can be stored in air-tight containers, if made before the house-raising date. They keep well...provided they stay uneaten.

ASSEMBLING THE HOUSE

Find a base for your gingerbread house. It can be a serving tray, cookie sheet or jelly roll pan (upside down if necessary), a piece of plywood, a bread board or plastic cuttng board. It is important that the base be able to support the weight of the house and decorations—up to several pounds—and be large enough to allow adequate space for landscaping and decorations—14" x 17" is probably the minimum size.

Icing is the substance that glues the walls of the gingerbread house together. Here is the recipe for the basic white icing "glue":

ICING

2 egg whites	Food coloring (food color paste or
1 box confectioners' sugar	liquid)
1 teaspoon lemon extract	

Separate the eggs, and place the whites in a medium-sized mixing bowl. (You will not be using the yolks. Store them in a small, covered dish.) Beat the whites lightly with an electric mixer or wire whisk. Add the confectioners' sugar and lemon extract. Stir with a wooden spoon until the icing is thick but smooth.

Use plain white icing for joining house parts together. Spoon half the mixture into a pastry bag fitted with a small, plain round tip. Put a rubber band on the top end of the pastry bag to keep the icing contained. Twist the top of the pastry bag to push the icing down towards the tip. If you have a metal cake decorator, spoon the icing in until it's half full and push the icing down with the plunger. Practice making an even bead along the base or on the table. A trial bead of icing should keep its shape as it comes out of the tip. It takes a bit of practice and strength to squeeze the stiff icing out evenly. If it's too loose it won't harden quickly and assembling the house sections will be more difficult. If it is too loose, return the icing to the bowl and add more sugar. If it's too stiff, it won't go through the tip at all. In this case, return the icing to the bowl and add lemon juice a drop at a time. Keep the remaining mixture in a plastic bag so that it does not harden.

Parchment Paper Decorators

Individual parchment paper decorators are easy to make and allow you greater flexibility in decorating. Using them alleviates the need to decorate with one color at a time: you can make a decorator for each color and use them in any order you'd like.

Cut a piece of parchment paper about 8" long. Roll it up to form a tight cone and tape it in place. Cut the tip off, making the size of the opening correspond to the kind of icing bead you'll want. A small cut across the tip will make a plain line. A many-pointed or "star" tip will make a fluted icing bead.

Spoon some icing into the decorator and fold over the top to close it. Squeeze carefully as you decorate, so as not to squeeze the icing out the top.

Joining the Walls

When the gingerbread is ready, arrange the four walls of the house on the table next to the base. Decide where the house will be placed on the base, depending on your decoration scheme. Hold the pastry bag or cake decorator and carefully make an even bead along the four edges of the two side walls where they will join the two end walls. A helper is useful for holding up the walls while you are working, but not essential. The icing must be stiff enough to set quickly.

Stand up one side and one end wall letting the icing make a joint. Hold for one minute to allow the icing to set a bit. Stand up the other side wall and join it to the end wall. Hold briefly. Join the remaining end to the icing beads along the side wall edges.

Check that the house is square—all walls parallel to outside edges of base. Carefully tie lengths of string around the four walls at the top and bottom of the walls. Make a bead of icing all around the base of the house to secure it to the base. Add another thin bead of icing along the inside of the wall joints to make it doubly secure—particularly if you plan to transport the finished house any distance. Be careful not to bump the walls when making the inside bead.

Spoon the icing into your pastry bag or cake decorator

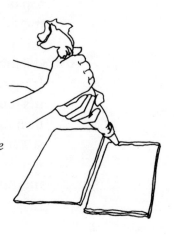

Squeeze beads of icing along the vertical edges of the wall pieces

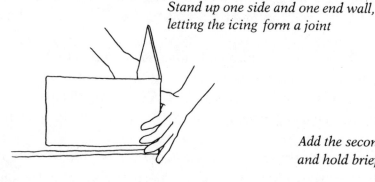

Stand up one side and one end wall, letting the icing form a joint

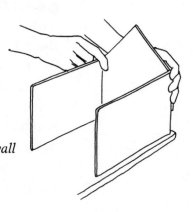

Add the second side wall and hold briefly

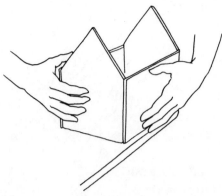

Join the remaining end wall to the other three, and check that the house is square

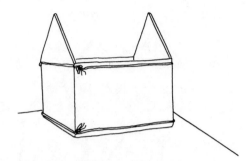

Tie lengths of string around the walls to secure them while they set

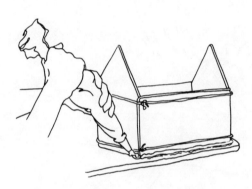

Run an icing bead around the base of the house

Make a thick bead of icing between the two roof pieces and push them together

Adding Doors and Shutters

After the walls have set for a few minutes, put shutter pieces and doors in place with beads of icing. Shutters can go in window holes, angled out or flat against the walls. Apply a bead of icing to the edges and hold in place until the joint seems secure. The door can be left open or shut. When open, secure it to the base with a bead of icing applied at the bottom.

Raising the Roof

Arrange the roof pieces smooth side up, side by side with 1/8" space between them. Make a bead of icing along the space and push the pieces together to make a joint. This will be the roof's peak.

Make a bead of icing around the top of the end walls and across the top of the side walls where the roof will sit.

Pick up the two roof pieces and place them carefully on the house, centering the overhanging edges all around. Hold in place for a minute while the icing joints harden.

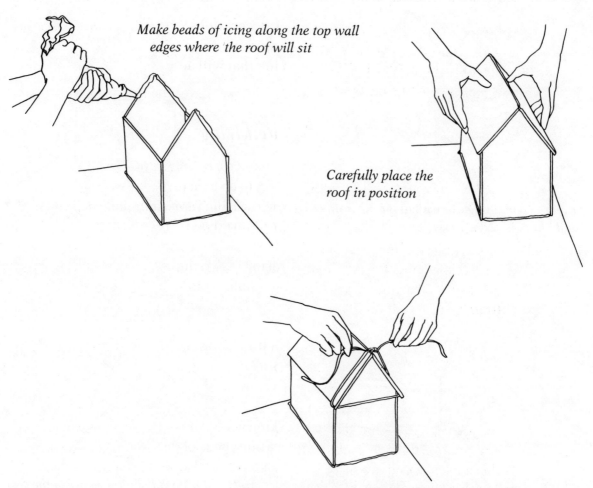

Make beads of icing along the top wall edges where the roof will sit

Carefully place the roof in position

Tie a string around each overhanging end of the roof to secure it while it sets

Tie a string around each end where there is an overhang—knotting it at the roof's peak. Carefully remove the string when the icing has set.

Your house is up! You'll find that it's surprisingly sturdy, so relax and enjoy decorating.

DECORATING

No gingerbread house is complete without loads of decoration—candies, nuts, coconut—whatever you can think of. In order to attach these finishing touches, you need to mix some glaze, which will serve as the "glue."

GLAZE

2 egg whites
Juice from 1/2 lemon

1 cup confectioners' sugar

Stir all the ingredients together in a small bowl until the mixture is creamy. With a small brush, apply it to any flat areas of the gingerbread house where you want to attach decorations. The glaze will be sticky enough so that you can add lots of ground nuts, coconut, colored sugar, sprinkles or small candies—anything that will add color, texture and additional flavor to your house.

Colored Icing

The icing remaining in the pastry bag or cake decorator can be re-mixed with what was set aside. If you expect to do a lot of decorating, mix another batch. For a variety of colors, divide the icing into small bowls and add the color of your choice—a little bit at a time. Food color paste has a range of more intense colors than the liquid drops, and it doesn't change the consistency of the icing. Drops of food coloring may require more sugar to keep the icing stiff. Remember that you can combine colors—either liquid or paste— to make different ones:

> Red and yellow = orange
> Red and blue = purple
> Blue and yellow = green

Use one color at a time for making icicles or swirls, trimming windows and doors, edging a path or decorating the roof. Each house described in this book has individual decorating ideas, but use your imagination as well. That's half the fun.

Stick rows of candies into the icing along the roof peak, around the windows and around the base. Position gingerbread trees, animals and people around the house. Stand two-dimensional figures—flat cookies of peo-

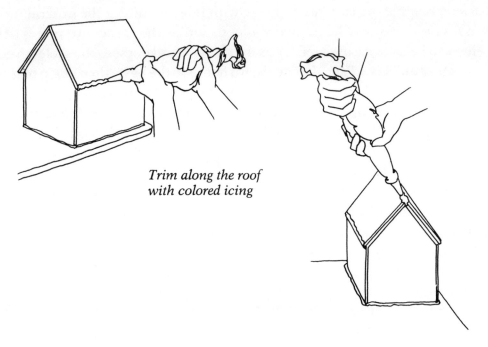

Trim along the roof with colored icing

ple and trees—in little mounds of icing. If necesary, prop them up until they've hardened in place.

Brush the glaze mixture onto any flat surfaces that you decide to decorate with a small, soft brush. Then sprinkle ground nuts, coconut, candy sprinkles or granulated sugar over the newly glazed surface.

Your house is finished—sparkling with color and texture. Decorate lots of extra cookies to go with your house—they get eaten first—but don't hesitate to enjoy sharing your creation with your friends after you've admired it for a while. You can always make another! If you really want to keep it, though, it will last for two months just as is—perfect for the Thanksgiving to Christmas holiday season.

HUMIDITY AND A CARDBOARD SKELETON

The success of a gingerbread house depends on the strength of the individual pieces. They should be of a uniform thickness and thoroughly cooled before you begin to assemble the house. High humidity may keep your cookie pieces from hardening sufficiently. A short warming and drying in the oven may help—then cool again.

If you plan to transport the house some distance, or if the weather seems particularly humid, you might want to build a cardboard skeleton to help support the house. Cut out all the pattern pieces in cardboard. (The corrugated kind is light and keeps its shape.) Cut the house pieces $1/8''$ smaller on all sides. This will allow the cardboard pieces to fit inside the gingerbread parts. Cut off any overhang on the cardboard roof pieces, and be sure to cut out all the doors and windows as well.

Assemble the cardboard pieces with tape, following the general directions for the style of house that you're making. (The cardboard pieces don't have to be handled as carefully as the gingerbread ones, so the skeleton goes together quickly.) Tape the cardboard house to the base, then begin to make the gingerbread house—following the usual directions. The cardboard skeleton will help support the gingerbread pieces as you work. Stand the wall pieces up and then fit the roof pieces on top of the cardboard. The gingerbread pieces can be attached with icing beads to the cardboard house as well as to each other.

For a final decorative touch—and so that the cardboard will not be visible—you can cut and fit pieces of colored paper, acetate, or foil in the door and window openings. Cut the paper a little larger than the opening and tape each piece to the cardboard before you put the gingerbread part over it. Your house will sparkle all the more and it will be as sturdy as the real thing!

3

HANSEL & GRETEL COTTAGE

Hansel and Gretel got into a lot of trouble nibbling at that magical house in the woods, but this cottage inspired by the story will cause nothing but smiles of delight. The witch's little house is a very simple project that really brings the fairy tale to life—and it is so easy to make that you will probably spend more time decorating it than actually building it. Use your own favorite candies to decorate the house, and turn it into a treat that no child can possibly resist nibbling.

The cottage, which resembles a Cape Cod-style house, is made of vanilla cookie dough. Its prominent chimney will certainly remind children of the witch heating up her oven to cook Hansel!

Have the following ingredients and materials on hand before you start your cottage:

INGREDIENTS

Vanilla Cookie Dough: one batch is plenty for the cottage and all the characters (See p. 13.)

Icing: white for assembly (See p. 17.)

Food color or paste

Glaze (See p. 20.)

Ground nuts for ground covering

Small gumdrops for roof and chimney decorations

Black and red raspberry candy drops

Red licorice

Colored sprinkles

Other candies of your choice

MATERIALS

Paper pattern pieces, cut out and labeled (See p. 10.)

Base on which to build cottage (at least 11" x 14")

Cake decorator or pastry bag

Brush for glaze

String

Mix and roll out your dough, cut out the paper pattern pieces and bake the gingerbread parts according to the basic instructions found on pp. 10-16. When all the cottage parts have been baked and thoroughly cooled, it is time to start assembling the house.

ASSEMBLING THE HOUSE

Walls

Place gingerbread pieces with smooth side down. Make a bead of icing on the vertical edges of the four walls where they will join together at the corners. Start by connecting the back wall and the left side wall. Prop them up with tin cans if necessary until you get the rest of the walls attached. Place the walls on the base in their final position, and continue the assembly by attaching the right side wall and the front wall (with the door opening).

Tie two pieces of string around the walls—one each at the top and bottom. Secure the cottage to the base with a bead of icing along the bottom outside edge. For extra stability you can add a bead along the inside edge as well. With a moistened finger, smooth the icing along the outside joints before it hardens. Fill in any cracks in the joints with more icing. The walls will assemble and set quite easily if the icing is stiff enough; it shouldn't take more than a minute or two to harden. If the icing does not set, add more confectioners' sugar and begin over.

Chimney

Assemble the chimney upside down on its flat edges. First place the pieces on the table, smooth side down. Make beads of icing along the vertical edges. Join the four pieces using the same method you used for the walls. Tie a string around the chimney and set it aside to allow the icing to harden.

Roof

Place the two roof pieces—smooth side up—side by side lengthwise, leaving a 1/8" space between them. Make a bead of icing along the space, and press the pieces together to make a joint. Make a bead of icing along the two gabled ends of the house and along the top edge of the two sides. Carefully lift the two roof pieces together and set them in place. Hold in place for a minute or two until the icing has set, then tie lengths of string around both roof ends to secure them. Allow the roof to set before adding the chimney, but in the meantime you can work on the decorating.

DECORATING

With a pencil, lightly sketch a pathway from the door to the edge of the base. Brush glaze along the path and generously apply the colored sprinkles over the glazed area. (The glaze holds the sprinkles in place.)

Put a little dab of icing on the bottoms of red and black raspberry drops and place them along the front and side edges of the base and along the front wall of the cottage.

Apply a dab of icing to the bottoms of gumdrops and place them along the edge of the pathway, forming a border along the sprinkle path.

Glaze the areas on both sides of the pathway and sprinkle ground nuts to cover the exposed base.

Pile loose candies on the nut-covered yard to add more colorful details and more treats to eat.

In order to help Hansel, Gretel, the witch, and the cat stand up, you must first scrape away a small area of the ground nuts with your finger. Spread a thick line of icing on the exposed base and set the cookies into the icing. If necessary, prop them until they harden in place.

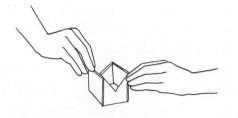

Assemble the chimney upside down, on its flat edges

Gently place the chimney in the center of the roof

Erecting the Chimney

Remove the strings from around the chimney and roof ends. Place the chimney in the center of the roof. Make an icing bead along the joint where the chimney meets the roof and hold in place momentarily, until set.

More Decorating Hints

Make a bead of icing along the top edges of the roof and chimney. Place small gumdrops or other candies into the icing before it hardens.

Make a bead of icing along the lower edge of the front and back of the roof and set licorice sticks into it. Hold a few moments to set.

Glaze roof and chimney and cover with colored sprinkles.

Icing Decoration

Divide the remaining icing into $1/3$ and $2/3$ parts. In a bowl add yellow food color or paste to the larger batch of icing and mix well. In a smaller bowl, add red food color or paste to the rest of the icing and mix well. Clean the pastry bag or cake decorator. Use only one color of icing at a time, moving on to the next color only after finishing with the first.

Use yellow icing and a medium tip for decorating around the curved windows and around the door trim; making eyes for Hansel and Gretel; along the corner edges; around the witch's hat.

Use red icing and a fine tip for the witch's eyes—and her cat's as well—and for all other trim on them; along the corner edges of the house; around the chimney.

Remember to go slowly while decorating, and think about the next step. You might even want to take a cookie break and help Hansel contemplate his fate before moving on to the next color or candy.

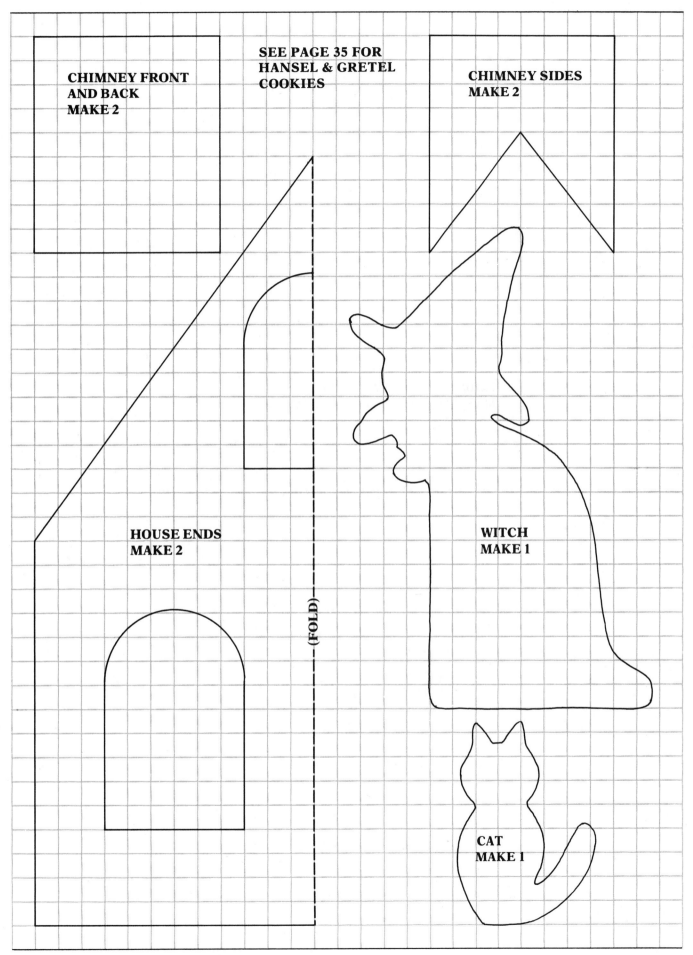

CHIMNEY FRONT
AND BACK
MAKE 2

SEE PAGE 35 FOR
HANSEL & GRETEL
COOKIES

CHIMNEY SIDES
MAKE 2

HOUSE ENDS
MAKE 2

(FOLD)

WITCH
MAKE 1

CAT
MAKE 1

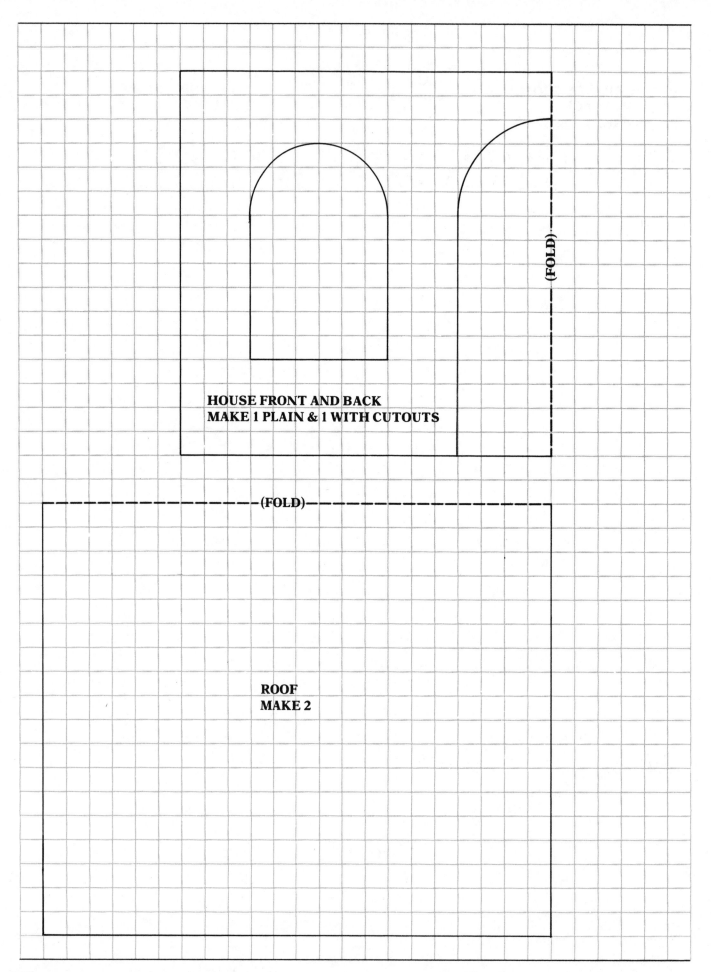

**HOUSE FRONT AND BACK
MAKE 1 PLAIN & 1 WITH CUTOUTS**

(FOLD)

(FOLD)

**ROOF
MAKE 2**

4

SCHOOLHOUSE

This quaint, one-room schoolhouse is actually a charming variation on the Hansel & Gretel cottage, substituting a bell tower for the chimney and featuring a big double door, open and welcoming. It's the perfect project to ease children's back-to-school blues.

Like the cottage, the schoolhouse is a simple structure with a gable roof, placing the emphasis on decoration rather than assembly. Chocolate dough is a nice choice for this structure. The letter and number cookies on the roof, as well as some of the children, can be made from the vanilla dough to add contrasting color and flavor.

If you use a large base, there will be room for a whole schoolyard full of boy and girl cookies waiting for the bell in the tower to ring and begin the school day.

Have the following ingredients and materials on hand before beginning the schoolhouse:

INGREDIENTS

Chocolate Cookie Dough: one batch is enough for the schoolhouse and some children (See p. 13.)

Vanilla Cookie Dough: $1/2$ batch will make several boy and girl cookies (but a whole batch will ensure that there are plenty to eat) (See p. 13.)

Icing: white for assembly (See p. 17.)

Red, yellow and green food color or paste for decoration

Glaze (See p. 20.)

Ground nuts for schoolyard

Candy for decoration (gumdrops, raspberry drops, jelly beans, red hots or other favorite varieties)

MATERIALS

Paper pattern pieces, cut out and labeled (See p. 10.)

Base for the schoolyard, at least 11" x 14"

String

Cake decorator or pastry bag

Brush for glaze

Mix and roll out your dough, cut out the paper pattern pieces and bake the gingerbread parts according to the basic instructions found on pp. 10-16. When you have baked and cooled all the schoolhouse parts and a classroom's worth of boys and girls, you are ready to assemble and decorate the house.

ASSEMBLING THE HOUSE

Walls

To raise the walls of the schoolhouse, follow exactly the instructions for assembling the Hansel & Gretel cottage. When deciding how to place the building on its base, remember to leave room for the schoolyard.

Bell Tower

Like the chimney on the Hansel & Gretel house, the bell tower should be assembled separately and left to harden. Follow the instructions for the chimney, and then add the bell tower roof.

Bell Tower Roof

The bell tower roof is a pyramid. Place the pieces on a flat surface, smooth side down, and make a bead of icing along each edge of each piece. Put all four pieces together and hold them until they are somewhat set. Then tie lightly with string and allow to harden. Smooth any excess icing along the joints.

Roof

Again, the roof of the schoolhouse is just like that of the cottage. Follow the cottage instructions for assembling and attaching it.

Further Assembly

After you have removed the strings securing the house walls, make beads of icing along the two vertical edges of the front door opening. Stand up the two door pieces on either side. Secure them along their bottom edges with beads of icing. Apply icing to the backs of the letter and number cookies and carefully attach them to the front wall over the door, and on the roof. Hold them gently until they stick firmly.

Trees

You still have time, while the roof sets, to make a few three-dimensional trees. Take a tree and slice it in half lengthwise. Make a bead of icing down the length of another whole tree and set the halved tree into the icing. Hold

Assemble the bell tower roof like a pyramid

Using icing, attach the number and letter cookies

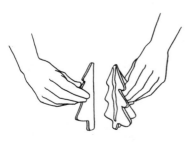

Make three-dimensional trees by adding tree halves on either side of a whole tree cookie

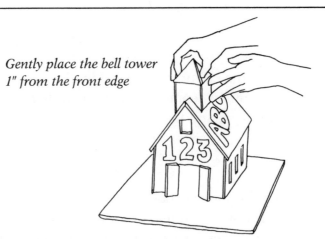

Gently place the bell tower 1" from the front edge

to secure. Repeat this procedure on the other side of the tree. Make half a dozen trees, and set them aside to harden while you continue the construction of the building.

Adding the Bell Tower

Untie the strings around the roof and bell tower. Place the bell tower base against the roof about 1" back from the front edge and make a bead of icing around it where it meets the roof. Smooth off the excess icing before it hardens.

Make a bead of icing along the top edge of the bell tower and place the bell tower roof carefully on top. Again, smooth off the excess icing.

Decoration

Any of the decorating hints offered in the Hansel & Gretel cottage section can be modified to suit the schoolhouse. To make candy edging, put a dot of icing on the bottoms of colored gumdrops or raspberry drops and space them evenly along the outside edge of the base.

Brush the base (schoolyard) with glaze and sprinkle ground nuts over the glazed surface, to create ground cover. Add a few loose gumdrops or jelly beans for color, if you wish.

To stand up the children, scrape away a small section of the ground nut surface—about as wide as the base of the cookie—and make a thick bead of icing in the space. Stand the cookies in the icing, propping them until set if necessary. (Small film canisters work very well as props.) Stand up any additional cookies, such as trees or dogs, in the same way.

Icing Decoration

Divide the remaining icing into thirds, placing it in three small bowls. Mix a different food color or paste (red, yellow and green) into each bowl, adding it a tiny bit at a time until you get the shade you like.

Clean the pastry bag or cake decorator and use it for one color at a time—remember, each time you switch colors, you'll have to clean the pastry bag again, so think carefully about where you'll want to use each color before you switch to a new one. Use a smaller tip on the pastry bag or decorator for the decorative colored icing.

Make yellow beads of icing along the bell tower roof joints, along the wall joints of the bell tower, along the ends of the gables, underneath the roof eaves, along the main wall joints, and around the front doors.

Make beads of red icing along the peak of the main roof and where the bell tower roof meets the tower. Decorate by sticking red hots into the icing before it hardens. You can also use the red icing for eyes on the boy, girl, and dog cookies.

Make green beads of icing around the windows and add green decoration to the number and letter cookies.

Add any additional icing decoration and candies that you like (remember to decorate the cookies so they have real personality), and you're finished! School is in session.

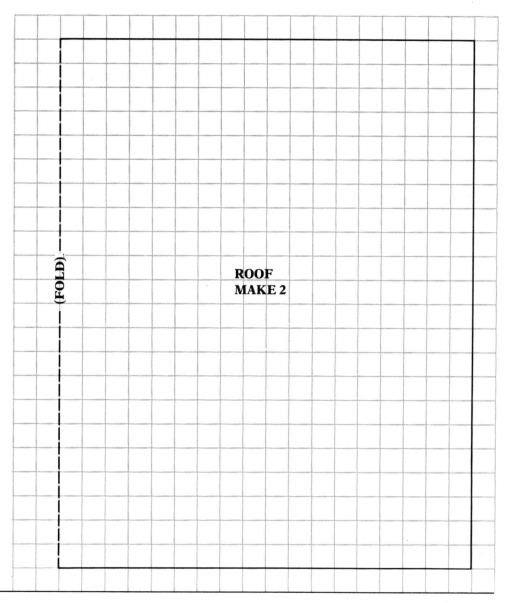

(FOLD)

ROOF
MAKE 2

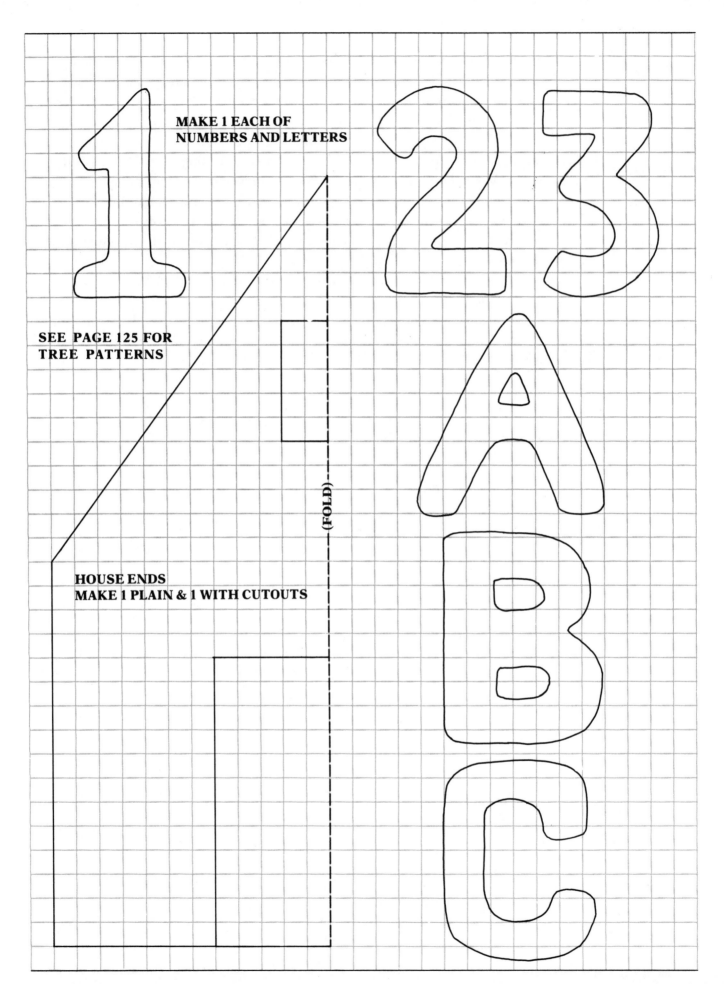

MAKE 1 EACH OF
NUMBERS AND LETTERS

SEE PAGE 125 FOR
TREE PATTERNS

(FOLD)

HOUSE ENDS
MAKE 1 PLAIN & 1 WITH CUTOUTS

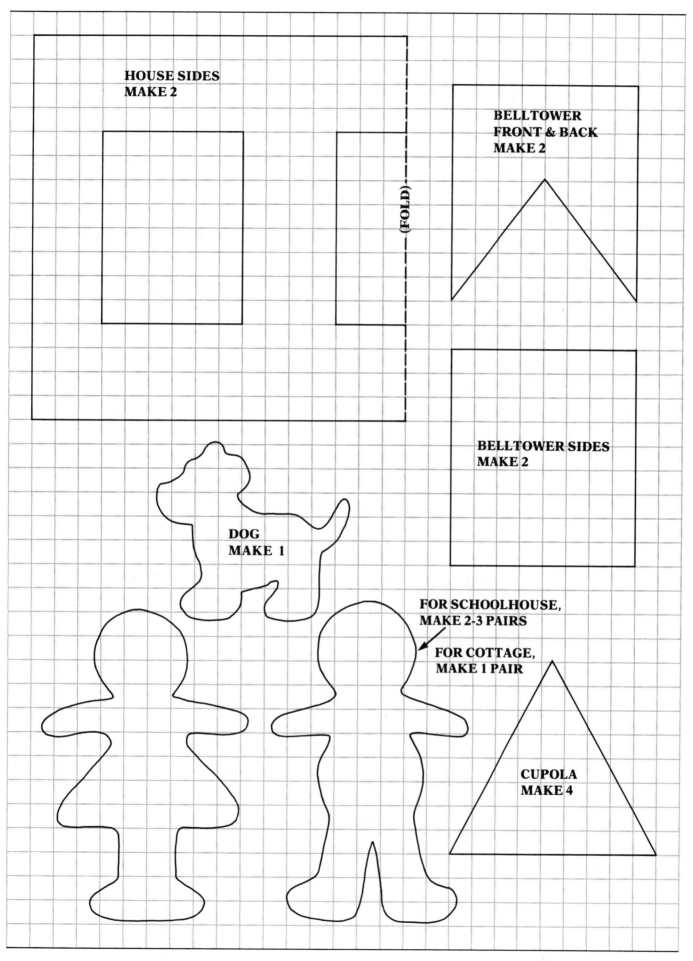

HOUSE SIDES
MAKE 2

(FOLD)

BELLTOWER
FRONT & BACK
MAKE 2

BELLTOWER SIDES
MAKE 2

DOG
MAKE 1

FOR SCHOOLHOUSE,
MAKE 2-3 PAIRS

FOR COTTAGE,
MAKE 1 PAIR

CUPOLA
MAKE 4

5

SALTBOX HOUSE

Enjoy a bit of Colonial America with the gingerbread saltbox house. The saltbox, built by early settlers, was an example of "solar" designing. The front wall always faced south for full exposure to the sun, while the north wall at the back was low, protected from the elements by a long, sloping roof. A large central chimney and fireplaces heated the house in winter months. Lots of these saltboxes can still be found in the towns of New England—and they're just as appreciated for their efficiency nowadays as when they were first constructed!

The shed-roofed back porch is perfect for storing produce from the attached vegetable garden. A wagon and horses, a picket fence and a border of icing flowers complete the scene.

When making the saltbox house, have the following ingredients and material handy:

INGREDIENTS

Basic Gingerbread Dough: one
   batch (See p. 12.)
Icing: one batch (See p. 17.)
Green food color or paste for
   mixing decorative icing
Glaze (See p. 20.)

Chocolate sprinkles
Green sprinkles
Gumdrops and other assorted
   candies (red hots, raspberry
   drops, Lifesavers, mints)
Rolled oats

MATERIALS

Paper pattern pieces cut out and
   labeled (See p. 10.)
Base for structure, at least 14" x
   17"
String

Cake decorator or pastry bag and
   assorted tips
Brush for glaze
Wax paper or parchment paper

Mix and roll out your dough, cut out the paper pattern pieces and bake the gingerbread parts according to the basic instructions found on pp. 10-16. When all the house parts have been baked and cooled, along with any people and animal cookies you decide you'll want to add later, it's time to assemble the saltbox.

ASSEMBLING THE HOUSE

Place the four main walls smooth side down on a flat work surface and make beads of icing along each of the vertical edges. Carefully place the house on its base, making sure to allow room for the back porch and vegetable garden. The front yard can be shallow. Stand up a side wall and an end wall, joining them together with the icing. Prop them up if necessary, while you attach the other side and end walls in the same manner. Tie the structure with two lengths of string while the icing is hardening, and make a bead of icing along the groundline to secure the house to its base. Allow to sit until the icing has thoroughly hardened.

Porch

Place the porch pieces smooth side down and make icing beads along the vertical edges. Untie the strings around the house walls and make a bead of icing along the two corners of the back wall where the porch will be attached. (Scrape away a bit of the groundline icing at the corners if it is in the way.) Stand up the two side walls and the back wall of the porch, holding or propping them while the icing sets a bit. Fill in any gaps in the icing and smooth away any excess with a moistened finger. Finally, add a bead of icing along the porch groundline to secure it to the base.

Chimney

It is a good idea to assemble the chimney upside down, on its flat edges. Place the chimney pieces smooth side down, and make beads of icing along all of the vertical edges. Carefully assemble the pieces, using the same method you used for the walls. Hold them carefully until they are somewhat set, and then tie string around the chimney and smooth any excess icing from the joints. Set it aside while you attach the roofs of the house and porch.

Roofs

Place the front and back sections of the main roof side by side—smooth side up this time—with $1/8''$ space between them. Make a bead of icing along the space and push the two pieces together, forming a joint.

Make beads of icing along the gable ends and the top edges of the front and back walls. Carefully pick up the joined roof pieces and put them in place on the house, holding them for a moment. Tie lengths of string, one at each end of the house, to secure the roof until thoroughly set.

Add the two side walls of the porch to the back wall of the house

Assemble the chimney upside down, on its flat edges

Place porch roof in position

*Secure the chimney with
a bead of icing*

Untie the strings from the ends of the main roof. Make a bead of icing along the top edges of the porch pieces and along the back wall of the house where the porch roof will join it. Place the roof on top of the porch, right up against the house wall. Make a bead of icing along the joint of the main roof and shed roof.

Chimney

Gently place the chimney on the roof—right in the center. Make a bead of icing where the chimney meets the roof. Smooth any excess icing with your moistened finger, filling in any gaps that may have formed. Your basic house is all assembled, and it's time to add the extra touches.

Fence, Wagon and Horses

Decorate the fence, wagon and horse pieces before you assemble them.

Change the tip on the cake decorator or pastry bag to a fine, plain one. Place the fence pieces, horse pieces and wagon pieces smooth side up on the table. Make beads of icing between the pickets of the fence. Decorate the wagon and horses with icing as well, adding eyes, mane and other details. Outline the windows and doors with beads of icing. Let all the icing harden before going on to assembly.

Fence

Assemble the picket fence in the same way as the porch walls. Place all the sections smooth side down on wax paper to protect the icing. Make icing beads along the vertical edges of the fence pieces, at the corners where the front of the house will meet the fence and along the base where the fence will

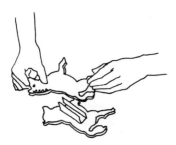

When the spreaders have hardened, carefully attach the second horse on top

Construct the wagon on its side

go. Attach the pieces to the house one at a time, propping them with tin cans while the icing hardens. Stand the front pieces of the fence in the bead of icing along the edge of the front yard. Stand up the gate piece so that it is half open.

Wagon

The wagon is constructed on its side. Carefully place the wagon pieces icing side down on a sheet of wax or parchment paper. On one side piece, make a bead of icing where the bottom and two end pieces will be placed. Also make a bead of icing on both ends of the bottom piece where it will join the end pieces. Stand the pieces in the beads of icing. Make sure the bottom and ends meet. Hold the pieces in place for a moment, and prop if necessary.

When the pieces have hardened in place, make a bead of icing along the exposed edges. Set the other half of the wagon in place, lining it up with the first half. Let the wagon harden completely before turning it upright.

Horses

The pair of horses is also constructed on its side. Carefully place one horse on the wax paper, icing side down. Make beads of icing along the *outer* edges of the two spreaders. Set them in place on the horse. Hold the spreaders for a moment and prop with a film canister if necessary. When the spreaders have thoroughly hardened (this should take about 5 minutes), make beads of icing along the exposed edges of the spreaders and carefully place the other horse on top. Be careful to line up the two halves. Hold the horses in place on their sides until they set. Let them harden completely and then you can turn them upright.

DECORATION

Decorating the House

Change the tip on your decorator or pastry bag to a finer one, and add thin decorative beads of white icing to the house. This draws attention to the unique lines of your saltbox, and lends a more "finished" air to the structure. Add the icing wherever it seems appropriate—along the roof peaks, around the chimney, under the eaves, around the windows and door—be generous.

Then brush the surfaces of the main roof and porch roof with glaze. Sprinkle it with rolled oats for added texture.

Path and Front Yard

Make a path leading from the gate to the front door, by brushing glaze along the base and covering it generously with colored sprinkles. You can make a straight path or a curvy one—just brush the glaze in the shape you want.

Garden

Put the remaining icing into a mixing bowl. Mix the green food coloring or food color paste into the bowl, adding it a bit at a time until you have a nice bright green.

Clean the pastry bag or cake decorator. Use a medium, fluted tip and green icing to make a decorative border around the garden and around the outside of the fence. Make rows of green icing for plants, varying the rows in thickness and height. Small, individual mounds of icing form heads of lettuce and bigger ones make bean plants or broccoli.

Now add rows of assorted candies for vegetables, herbs and flowers. Vary the height and patterns of your candy rows. Add a row of candy flowers around the front of the house for even more color.

When you've added as much garden as you want, brush glaze over the rest of the front and back yards. Cover the glaze with rolled oats and then dust with green sprinkles for a hint of grass.

Place the wagon and horses in the back yard—near the corner of the garden. Fill the wagon with oats and candy.

Step back and survey your work—it should be quite a colonial scene. Enjoy the bounty of your garden and the traditional charm of the decorated saltbox house.

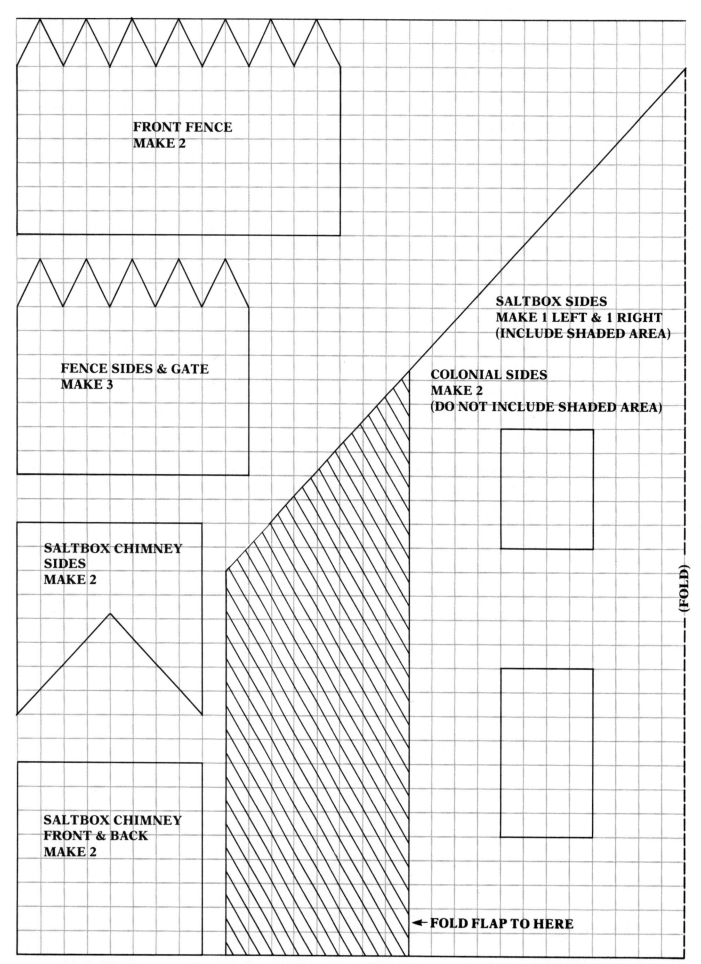

FRONT FENCE
MAKE 2

SALTBOX SIDES
MAKE 1 LEFT & 1 RIGHT
(INCLUDE SHADED AREA)

COLONIAL SIDES
MAKE 2
(DO NOT INCLUDE SHADED AREA)

FENCE SIDES & GATE
MAKE 3

SALTBOX CHIMNEY
SIDES
MAKE 2

(FOLD)

SALTBOX CHIMNEY
FRONT & BACK
MAKE 2

← FOLD FLAP TO HERE

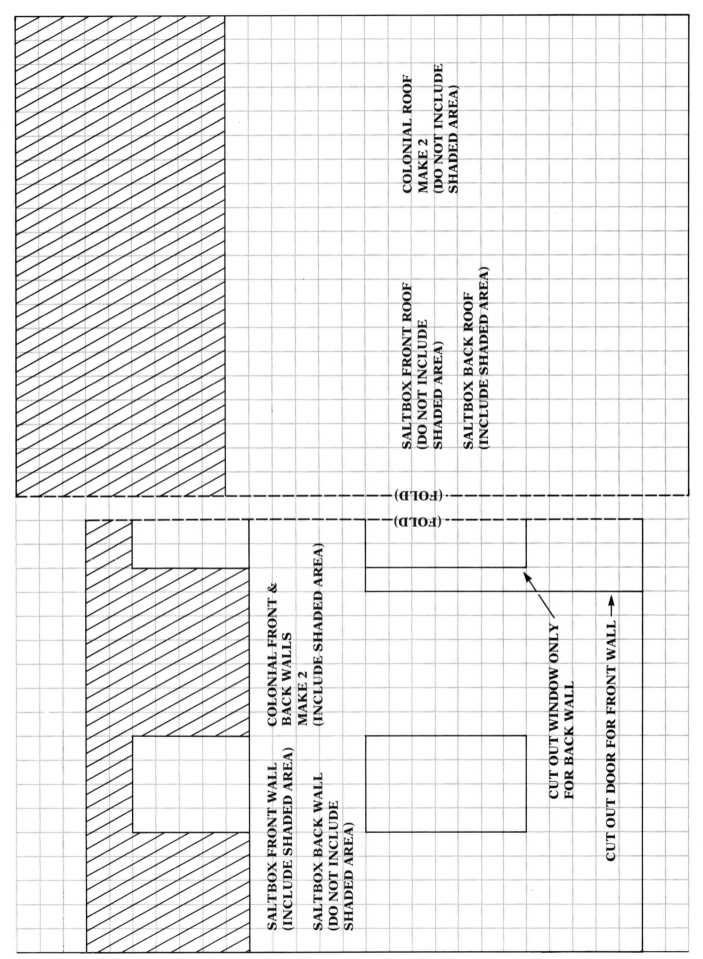

COLONIAL ROOF
MAKE 2
(DO NOT INCLUDE
SHADED AREA)

SALTBOX FRONT ROOF
(DO NOT INCLUDE
SHADED AREA)

SALTBOX BACK ROOF
(INCLUDE SHADED AREA)

(FOLD)

(FOLD)

COLONIAL FRONT &
BACK WALLS
MAKE 2
(INCLUDE SHADED AREA)

SALTBOX FRONT WALL
(INCLUDE SHADED AREA)

SALTBOX BACK WALL
(DO NOT INCLUDE
SHADED AREA)

CUT OUT WINDOW ONLY
FOR BACK WALL

CUT OUT DOOR FOR FRONT WALL →

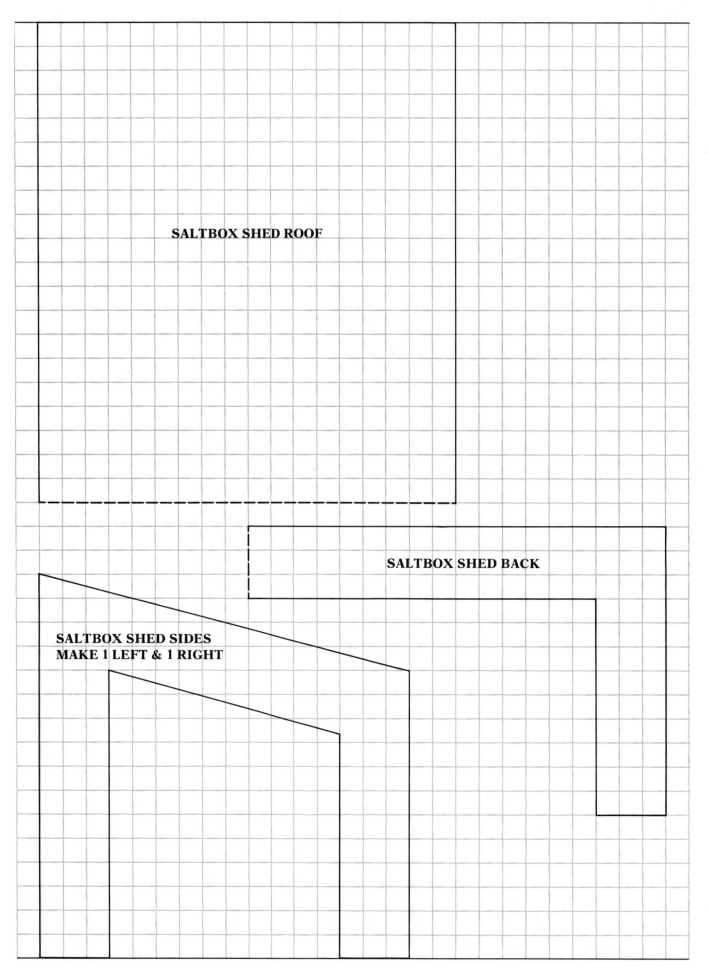

SALTBOX SHED ROOF

SALTBOX SHED BACK

SALTBOX SHED SIDES
MAKE 1 LEFT & 1 RIGHT

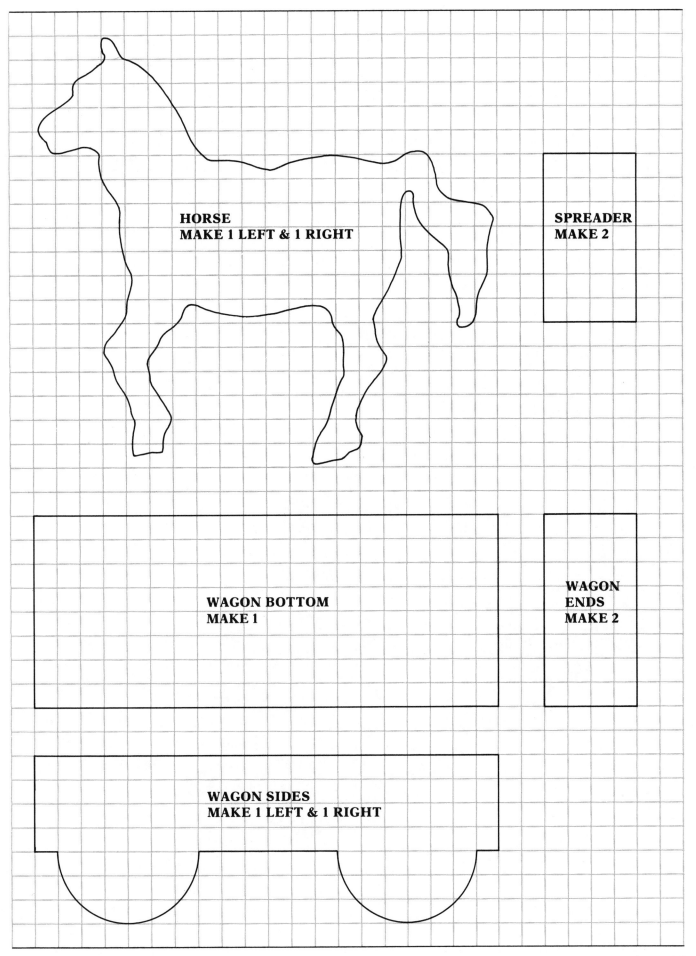

HORSE
MAKE 1 LEFT & 1 RIGHT

SPREADER
MAKE 2

WAGON BOTTOM
MAKE 1

WAGON ENDS
MAKE 2

WAGON SIDES
MAKE 1 LEFT & 1 RIGHT

6

COLONIAL HOUSE

The first colonists who came to this country from Holland, France, Spain and England brought their knowledge of architecture with them to the new world. The simple house now known as "Colonial" is one of the more practical and popular styles they introduced. Colonial houses can now be found dotting the countryside and villages along the New England seacoast.

This version of a Colonial features a semi-circular fanlight over the door, shutters around the windows, two dormers and a formal herb garden, lending lots of charm and character. It's not too complicated—just follow the directions step by step.

Before beginning the Colonial house have the following ingredients and materials handy:

INGREDIENTS

Basic Gingerbread Dough: one batch (See p. 12.)
Icing (See p. 17.)
Glaze (See p. 20.)
Small and large nonpareils, shredded coconut, green
sprinkles, slivered almonds, chocolate chips, raisins, gumdrops and/or your favorite candies or treats for the herb garden and flower box.

MATERIALS

Paper pattern pieces cut out and labeled (See p. 10.)
Cookie cutters for trees and flowers
Base for structure, at least 14" x 17"
String
Wax paper or parchment
Cake decorator or pastry bag with assorted tips
Brush for applying glaze

Mix and roll out your dough, cut out the paper pattern pieces and bake the gingerbread parts according to the basic instructions found on pp. 10-16. Be sure to bake plenty of extra bush, tree and flower cookies (see pp. 123-27 for patterns).

So you'll have shutters later, before baking the house parts, cut along the pattern of the windows, but leave the windows in place during the baking period. During the trimming stage, cut again around the windows and then cut each window down the middle, making the shutter pieces. After the full baking period is completed, cool slightly and then remove the shutter pieces. Cool thoroughly. (The door can be removed in a similar manner, so you can place it in an open position later, or you can leave it shut.)

ASSEMBLING THE HOUSE

Walls

Plan where your house will rest on its base. By centering it along the back edge, you will have a roomy front yard with garden space and room for paths, trees and bushes.

Lay the four wall pieces on the table with the smooth sides facing down. Make a bead of icing along the vertical edges of all four walls. (It is important to keep the icing stiff when joining the house parts.)

Stand the front wall and side wall together in position, joining them with the icing. Hold them a moment while they set, and then attach the other side wall and the back wall. Tie two lengths of string around the house—one at the base and one at the top. Make a bead of icing around the bottom of the house attaching it to the base. Smooth all iced joints with a moistened finger, filling in any gaps.

While the walls are setting, move on to build the dormers.

Dormers

Place the front piece of the dormer smooth side down on the table. Ice along the vertical edges. Then stand the two side pieces in place on top of the front piece, making sure the smooth sides are facing out. Hold each side piece for a moment, or prop with small spice containers if necessary.

Assemble the second dormer in the same way. (The dormer roofs will be added later, after the dormers are in place on the main roof.) The house walls should be sturdy by now, so it's time to add the main roof.

Roof

Place the two roof pieces side by side lengthwise, smooth sides facing up, with a 1/4" gap between them. Make a bead of icing between the two pieces and push them together to form a joint. Make a bead of icing along the gabled ends and the front and back edges of the house walls, where the roof will sit.

Carefully place the roof pieces in place. Hold them for a few moments. Tie two lengths of string around the gabled ends of the roof to hold the structure in place.

Flower Boxes

Place the front piece of the flower box smooth side down on the table. Make a bead of icing along the two vertical edges and one horizontal edge. Set the two side pieces and the bottom piece in place, holding each one for a mo-

Stand the two side pieces of the dormer on top of the front piece, smooth side out

Gently attach finished dormers to the roof

ment until partially set. Make sure you keep the smooth sides of the cookies facing outward.

Prop the sides of the flower box with small spice jars and let set. Now make the other flower box in the same way.

Shutters

Untie the strings around the walls. Separate the shutters—the longer ones are for the ground floor. With the smooth surface facing down, make a bead of icing down the middle of each shutter and set them in place next to each window.

Placing the Dormers

With the dormer still in its construction position, make a bead of icing along the angled side pieces and the base of the front. Carefully set the dormers in place, one at a time, spacing them about 2"-3" from the edge of the front roof.

Make a bead of icing along the joints where the dormers meet the roof. Tie a string around the roof, encompassing the dormers. Allow it to set for a while.

Placing the Flower Boxes

When the flower boxes are thoroughly set, make a bead of icing along the three back edges of the boxes and set them under the front windows. Soon you will be able to plant your flowers, but for now, let the pieces set. Prop them from underneath if necessary.

Dormer Roof

When the dormer has hardened in place, remove all strings from the roof. Repeat the same roofing procedure you followed for the main roof. Place the two dormer roof pieces side by side lengthwise, smooth side up. Leave a 1/8" space between them and make a bead of icing along the space. Push the two pieces together to form a joint.

Make a bead of icing along the top edges of the dormer. Carefully set the roof pieces in place. Ice along the joints where the dormer roof meets the main roof. Smooth the icing joints and fill in any gaps that may have formed.

The basic construction of the house is now complete, and the fun of decorating begins. Now is when the real character of your Colonial takes shape.

DECORATION

Divide the remaining icing equally into two small bowls. Slowly add red food color or paste to one bowl and green to the other, mixing until you reach shades you like.

Clean your decorator or pastry bag and fill it with red icing. Attach a plain, fine tip. Make an outline around the shutters, windows and door. Add the semi-circular window above the door entrance by drawing a half-circle and then making short, radiating lines forming the sections. Decorate some of the shrubs and trees with red icing as well.

Herb Garden

The herb garden should contain all of your favorite plants, formed from your favorite sweets. Bunches of raisins in rows, sunflower seeds, chocolate chips, colorful Lifesavers or slivered almonds are just a few of the possibilities. With a pencil, trace a circle in the center of the front yard, for the herb garden. You can trace around a juice can and large jar to make two concentric circles, if you wish, for the garden and path around it.

Make the path lead around the garden to the front door and out to the front edge of the base. Then decide how many sections you want in the herb garden and divide the inner circle accordingly.

Clean the decorator and fill it with the green icing. Using the plain, fine tip, make a thin bead of icing along the spokes of the herb garden and along the edges of the path. Set small nonpareils into the icing, forming an outside edging for the garden path. Then fill each section of the garden with candies, nuts or icing flowers made with a decorative tip. If you prefer ground nuts, you must first glaze the sections where you want them, to help glue them to the base. Small candies can be placed in bunches to create a bountiful garden. With a fine tip on your decorator, decorate the trees. With a medium, fluted tip, make a decorative border around the base and place raspberry drops in the icing.

It's time to fill the flower boxes with your favorite flowers—made from candies, of course. Set colorful gumdrops, Lifesavers or small, flower-

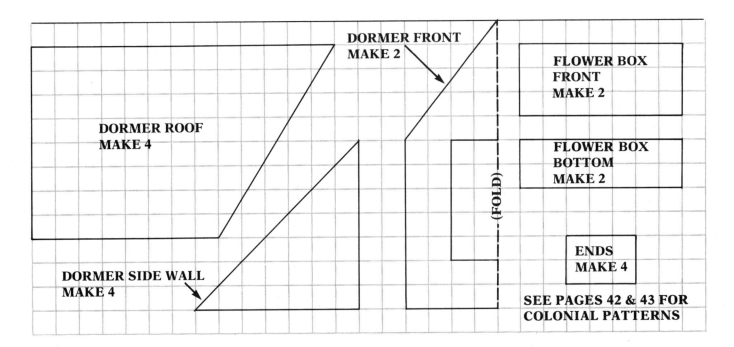

DORMER FRONT
MAKE 2

FLOWER BOX
FRONT
MAKE 2

DORMER ROOF
MAKE 4

FLOWER BOX
BOTTOM
MAKE 2

(FOLD)

ENDS
MAKE 4

DORMER SIDE WALL
MAKE 4

SEE PAGES 42 & 43 FOR
COLONIAL PATTERNS

shaped gingerbread cookies in place. A combination of treats adds color and variety.

Now make thin beads of icing along the paths and set larger nonpareils into them one by one, forming "stones."

Make thick beads of icing on the base and set the cookie shrubbery and trees in the yard. Use your judgment as to spacing. These can be propped with small jars if necessary. If you space four or five bushes and trees close together, you'll form a hedge.

Brush glaze on the main and dormer roofs and cover with coconut. Brush glaze all over the yard (wherever any of the base is still showing) and sprinkle it first with coconut and then with green sprinkles, forming a festive ground cover.

Review your handiwork—now is the time to add any finishing touches you see fit, and stand up any cookies you've been planning to add. To add these, scrape away patches of the ground cover and fill the space with a bead of icing. Stand the cookies in the icing and hold or prop until they're set.

Your house is now fit for colonists—even George Washington, should he happen to ride by needing a place to stay!

7

·•·•·•·•·•·•·•·•·

GOTHIC HOUSE

The dramatic Gothic farmhouse, with its steeply pitched roof, intersecting gables and imposing four-story tower, replicates a style popular in the northeastern United States in the mid-1800s—but you don't have to appreciate history to enjoy the startling effect once it's finished. The chocolate gingerbread dough is just right for the walls of this house, and vanilla dough contrasts well for the roof and tower. Purple and yellow decorative icing make eye-catching trim, and little silver candies complete the spooky Gothic look.

Have the following ingredients and materials handy before you start the Gothic house:

INGREDIENTS

Vanilla Cookie Dough: one batch will be enough for the tower and roof sections (See p. 13.)

Chocolate Cookie Dough: one batch will make the wall sections, with plenty left for individual cookies (See p. 13.)

Icing: white for assembly (See p. 17.)

Purple and yellow food color or paste for trim (or colors of your choice)

Glaze (See p. 20.)

Ground nuts for lawn

Candies for decoration: silver balls and your other favorites

MATERIALS

Paper pattern pieces cut and labeled (See p. 10.)

Base for the house, at least 16″ x 20″

String

Cake decorator or pastry bag and assorted tips

Brush for glaze

Skewer and ruler for making roof patterns

Mix and roll out your dough, cut out the paper pattern pieces and bake the gingerbread parts according to the basic instructions found on pp. 10-16. When you have baked and cooled all the Gothic house parts, along with a batch of people and pets to populate it when it's finished, it's time to begin assembling and decorating.

ASSEMBLING THE HOUSE

Walls

Before you raise the walls of your house, you must do a bit of architectural planning. Decide where you want the two wings of the house to be placed on the base. The tower will nestle right in the angle of the "L."

Place the wall sections smooth side down on a flat work surface. Make icing beads along the vertical edges of each wall section. Then stand up a side section and an end section on the base and join them together with the icing. Prop them up if necessary, while you attach the other side and end sections in the same manner. Tie a length of string around the walls near the top, and another near the bottom, to hold it while it sets. With a moistened finger, smooth the icing along the outside joints before it hardens.

The side L has only three walls, because there is an open end where it attaches to the main wing. Assemble the side wing about 2" away from where it will join the main wing. Apply beads of icing along the vertical edges as before. Stand the end and one side wall together, and then add the other side wall. Prop them up with cans until they harden. You can add a temporary cardboard end cut from the pattern piece, so that you can tie a length of string around the wing until it hardens.

When the two wings seem secure, untie the strings and remove the cardboard end. Move the side wing carefully to butt up against the main wing. Make beads of icing where the walls meet. Add a bead of icing along the bottom edge of the entire house, to secure it to the base. With a moistened finger, smooth the iced joints to remove any excess icing and fill in any gaps.

Your house is taking shape; just add the tower and roof and then you can start decorating.

Tower

Assemble the tower on its side. Place the three wall pieces and the two end pieces for the tower smooth side down on the table. Make a bead of icing along the four edges of one of the walls. Make beads of icing along all the edges where wall pieces will join end pieces. Stand up the pieces two at a time, keeping the end pieces on the outside of the side pieces. Prop the pieces from the outside with cans and from the inside with crumpled paper towels. Tie a string lengthwise around the box you have made. When the box has set, make a bead of icing around the exposed edge and put the fourth side carefully in place.

Allow the tower to set completely before you move it.

Tower Roof

The tower roof is a pyramid shape with four triangular pieces. Place the pieces smooth side down. Make beads of icing along the sides of each piece. Stand them up with two sides inside the other two sides, and hold them together until they set a bit. Then tie string lightly around the little roof so it can set completely, and smooth any excess icing from the joints.

Set the tower in place
and add icing where each
side meets the house

Set the side roof in place
fitting it around the tower
and against the main roof

Tower Assembly

Once the tower and tower roof have thoroughly set, you're ready to put them together and attach them to the house. Untie the string from the tower and stand it upright. Make a bead of icing along the top edge of the tower and gently set the roof in place. Let it set for a moment, and then set the whole tower structure in place where the two wings of the house meet. Carefully add a bead of icing where each side of the tower meets a wall of the house, and smooth any excess.

Front Roof

Place the two front roof sections side by side smooth side up, leaving 1/8" space between them. Make a bead of icing along the space and push the pieces together, forming a joint.

Make a bead of icing along the two gable ends and the top edges of the two side walls of the front wing. Carefully pick up the joined roof pieces and place them on the front wing of the house, easing the piece next to the tower into place. Hold them for a moment and then tie two lengths of string around the ends of the roof to secure it while it hardens.

Side Roof

Assemble the side roof in the same way you did the front roof, making an icing joint and pushing the two roof parts together. Remember to assemble the roof smooth side up. The slanted end on these pieces is where the side roof joins the front roof.

Make a bead of icing along the gable end of the side roof and along the top of the side walls. Pick up the two pieces and put them on the house, easing the piece next to the tower in place and butting the slanted end snugly up against the front roof. Make a bead of icing along the two joints where the side roof and the front roof meet. Smooth all the joints with your moistened finger. After it sets for a few minutes, the whole elaborate structure should be quite sturdy.

DECORATION

Lightly score the roof in a diamond pattern, using a skewer and ruler. Make parallel diagonal lines first in one direction and then the other, on both sides of both roof sections.

Divide the remaining icing into $2/3$ and $1/3$ portions and place it in two small bowls. Add yellow food coloring or paste to the bowl with the $1/3$ portion—a little at a time—until you create a shade you like. Then add red and blue food color or paste to the other bowl, mixing until you get a rich purple.

Clean the pastry bag or decorator and fit it with a thin, plain tip. Fill it with the purple icing. Remember that you'll have to clean it again before you use the yellow icing, so plan carefully all of the places you'll want to use purple—even on the separate cookies you made earlier. Ice the roof along the scored diamond pattern. With purple icing and a plain medium tip, make thicker beads along the vertical joints of the tower, under the eaves of the two roofs, along the peak of the tower roof and along the peaks of the two main roofs. Place little silver candy beads along the peaks. If you'd like your cookie people and animals to have a splash of color, use purple for eyes and clothing.

When you're certain you're done with the purple, clean the pastry bag or cake decorator and fill it with yellow icing. Carefully ice around all the windows and the door, and add more yellow anywhere else that needs a bit of brightness.

Brush glaze all over the exposed base and sprinkle it with ground nuts to create a yard. To stand your people and animal cookies in the yard, scrape away a patch of nuts with your finger and fill the space with a thick bead of icing. Stand the cookie in the icing and prop it up until it sets.

Ice the roof along the scored diamond patterns

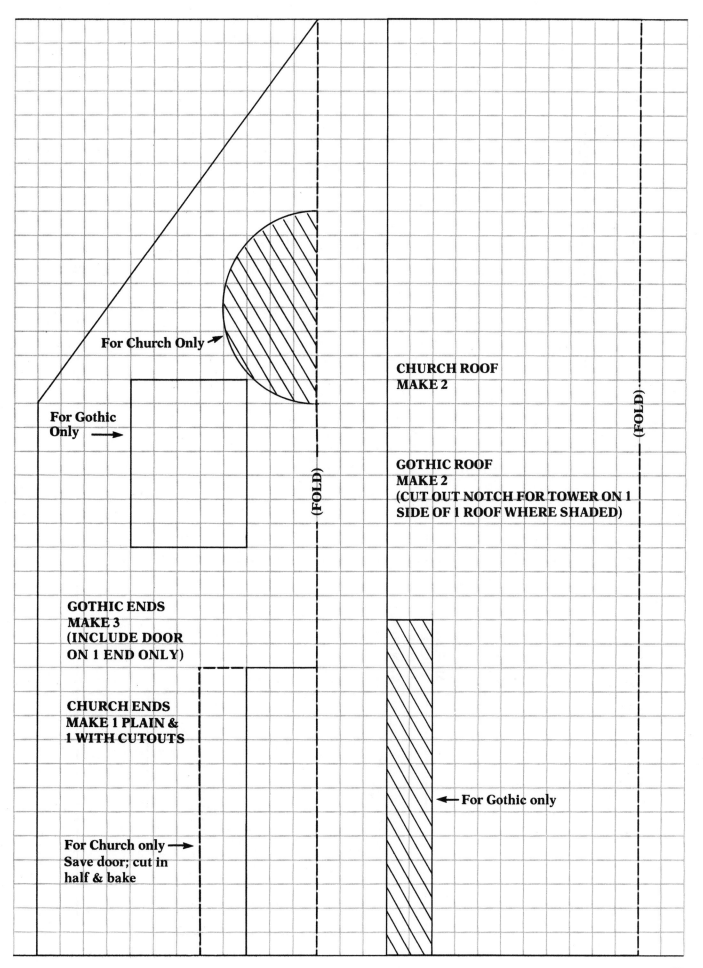

For Church Only

CHURCH ROOF
MAKE 2

For Gothic
Only

GOTHIC ROOF
MAKE 2
(CUT OUT NOTCH FOR TOWER ON 1
SIDE OF 1 ROOF WHERE SHADED)

(FOLD)

(FOLD)

GOTHIC ENDS
MAKE 3
(INCLUDE DOOR
ON 1 END ONLY)

CHURCH ENDS
MAKE 1 PLAIN &
1 WITH CUTOUTS

For Gothic only

For Church only
Save door; cut in
half & bake

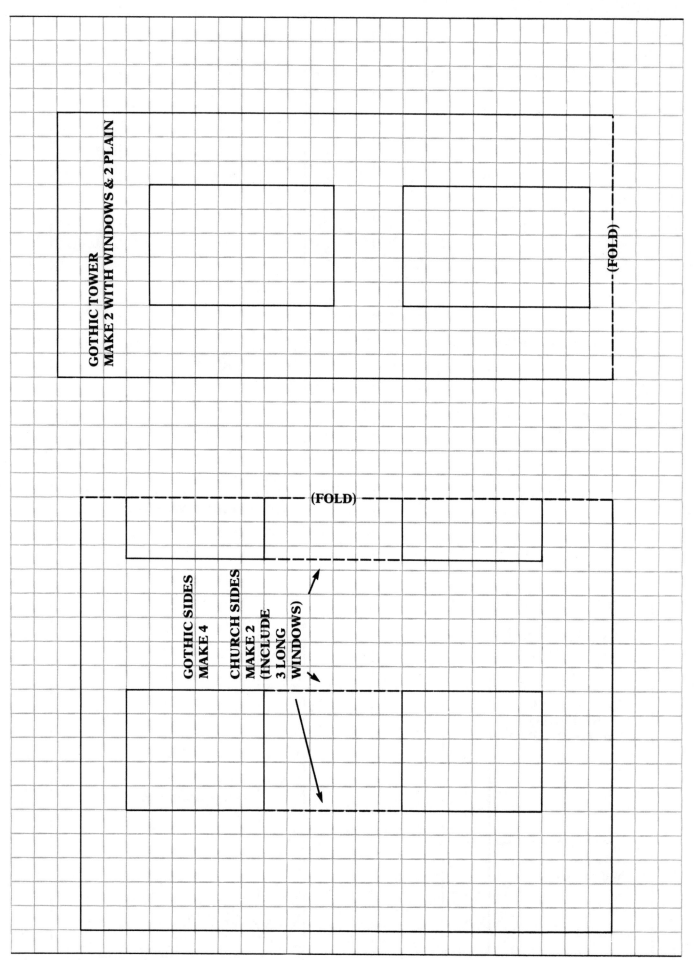

GOTHIC TOWER
MAKE 2 WITH WINDOWS & 2 PLAIN

(FOLD)

(FOLD)

GOTHIC SIDES
MAKE 4

CHURCH SIDES
MAKE 2
(INCLUDE
3 LONG
WINDOWS)

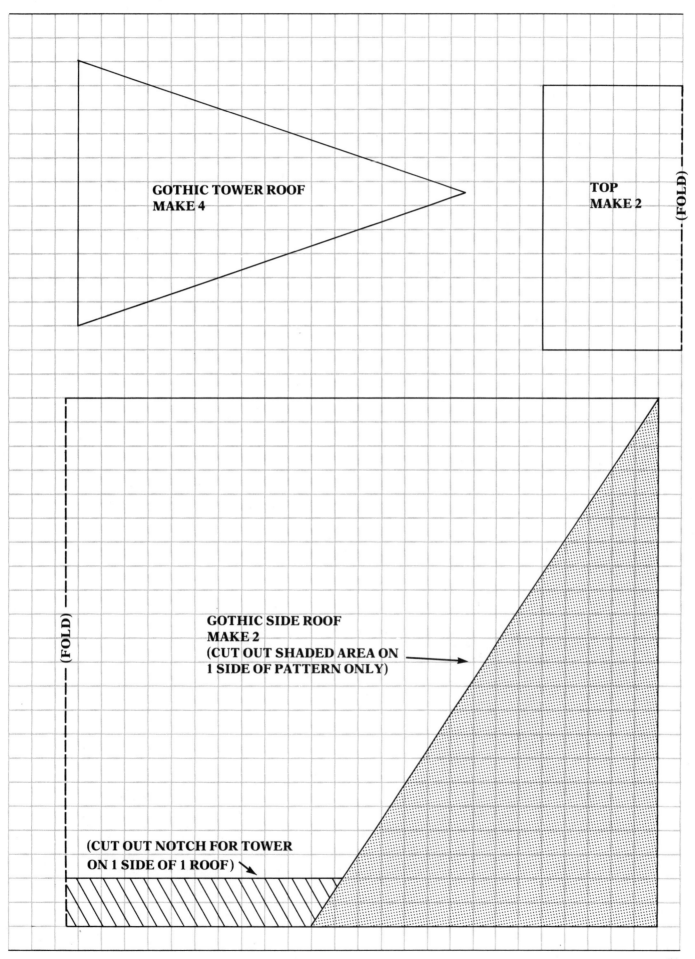

**GOTHIC TOWER ROOF
MAKE 4**

**TOP
MAKE 2**

(FOLD)

**GOTHIC SIDE ROOF
MAKE 2
(CUT OUT SHADED AREA ON
1 SIDE OF PATTERN ONLY)**

(FOLD)

**(CUT OUT NOTCH FOR TOWER
ON 1 SIDE OF 1 ROOF)**

8

CHURCH

I magine what a striking decoration this gingerbread church will make for a christening or an Easter celebration. With the addition of some seasonal "snow" made from coconut, it makes an unusual Christmas treat as well. Set in a large churchyard—complete with an eerie old cemetery enclosed by a rickety fence—the church includes some impressive details that are actually quite simple to create, such as an authentic-looking rose window. A steeple rises to an imposing height, and additional large windows and double doors offer a glimpse inside. The steeple is actually a variation on the tower designed for the Gothic house, so once you've constructed that one, the church is easy.

Before beginning construction of the church, have the following ingredients and materials close at hand:

INGREDIENTS

Vanilla Cookie Dough: one batch will be plenty for the church, tombstones and trees (See p. 13.)
Icing: white for assembly (See p. 17.)
Red food color or paste for window and door decoration
Glaze
Nonpareil candies (large box)

Multicolored Lifesavers
One red raspberry drop or large gumdrop (for steeple peak)
1 cup grated coconut
1 jar green sprinkles
1 box thin chocolate mints (such as After 8 variety)

MATERIALS

Paper pattern pieces cut out and labeled (See p. 10.)
Base for structure, at least 14" x 18"
String

Aluminum foil and wax paper
Cake decorator or pastry bag
Brush for glaze
Hammer (for crushing Lifesavers)

Mix and roll out your dough and cut out the paper pattern pieces according to the basic instructions found on pp. 10-16. Before baking the church parts, you'll have to prepare the beautiful "rose window" that gets baked in the front wall.

Rose Window

Crush 6 to 8 multicolored Lifesavers by placing them in a small, closed plastic bag and hammering them until they crumble to small, pebble-size bits. Set them aside. Before baking the front wall, slip a piece of lightly greased aluminum foil (greased side up) between the top half of the wall

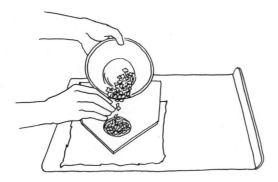

Fill the rose window opening with crushed Lifesavers

part and the baking sheet. Make sure that the foil completely fills the window opening. Bake as usual. During the last 5 to 7 minutes of baking time, generously sprinkle the crushed Lifesavers in the window opening. Cover the visible foil entirely with candy. As you continue baking, keep an eye on the rose window so as to avoid burning the candies. You'd better peek into the oven every two minutes or so. When the crushed candy has melted together, remove the baking sheet from the oven and cool the front wall piece thoroughly before removing it from the pan. Carefully lift the front wall piece and peel off the aluminum foil from the back.

When all of the pieces are baked and cooled, assembly of the church can begin.

ASSEMBLING THE CHURCH

Walls

Place the wall parts smooth side down and make beads of icing along each vertical edge. Stand the back and side walls together. Then stand the front wall, with the rose window, in place. Tie two lengths of string around the structure to secure it while drying. Smooth the icing along the outside joints before it hardens completely, using a moistened finger. Add more icing to fill in any gaps in the joints.

Make a bead of icing along the bottom of the structure to secure it to its base.

Steeple Base

Assemble the steeple base upside down on its flat edges. Make beads of icing along the vertical edges. Join the four pieces using the same method you used for the walls. Tie a string around the steeple base and set it aside to allow the icing to harden.

Steeple Roof

Place the four triangular pieces smooth side down. Make beads of icing along the two long edges of each piece. Assemble the four walls like a pyramid. A crushed paper towel formed into a cone and placed carefully inside the steeple roof adds support while the icing hardens. Tie a length of string around the steeple roof while it sets.

Church Roof

While you worked on the steeple, the church walls had a chance to set, and they are now ready for the addition of the roof. Place both roof pieces smooth side up side by side lengthwise, leaving a ⅛″ space between the two pieces. Make a thick bead of icing along the space and push the pieces together to form a joint. Make a bead of icing along the gabled ends of the church and along the top edges of the side walls. Place the roof pieces in position, holding them for a moment until they're somewhat set. Then tie strings around the overhanging roof edges and allow to set completely.

Trees

You still have time, while the roof sets, to make a few three-dimensional trees. Take a tree and slice it in half lengthwise. Make a bead of icing down the length of another whole tree and set the halved tree into the icing. Hold to secure. Repeat this procedure on the other side of the tree. Make half a dozen trees, and set them aside to harden while you continue the construction of the building.

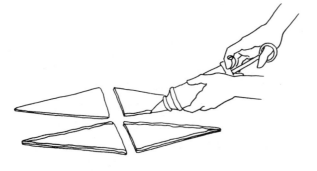

Apply icing beads along the side edges of the steeple

Hold the sides together until the steeple sets slightly

Make three-dimensional trees by adding tree halves on either side of a whole tree cookie

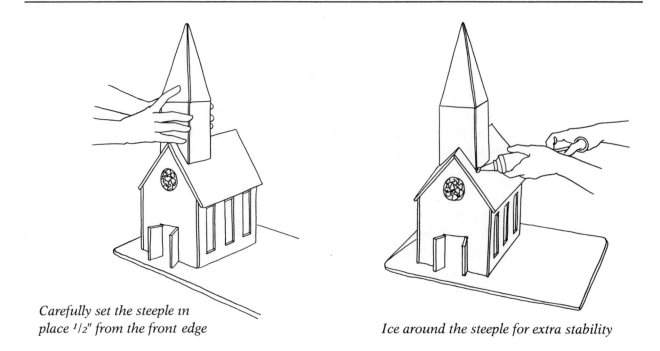

Carefully set the steeple in place ¹/2" from the front edge

Ice around the steeple for extra stability

Adding the Steeple

Both the steeple and the church should be thoroughly set by now, so remove all the strings. Carefully set the steeple base onto the church roof, ¹/2" back from the front wall. Ice along the joint where the steeple base meets the roof, smoothing away the excess icing, and let it stand to set.

When the steeple base is hardened into place, make a thin bead of icing along the top edge of the steeple and set the roof onto it, holding it in place for a moment. Smooth out any excess icing with your finger.

Door

Make a thin bead of icing along both sides of the church door opening and set the door pieces in place. Be sure to keep the smooth sides of the cookies facing out. The doors can be wide open or partially ajar, depending on your fancy. A bead of icing along the base of the doors will secure them to the base.

The church is fully assembled, awaiting your decorating touches.

DECORATION

Now it's time to add the character to your creation. With the white icing, make a bead along all the joints on the steeple, along the roof peak, and along the gabled ends of the church. Gently set the nonpareil candies into the icing, spacing them evenly but generously all along the iced joints.

Brush glaze on the roof and sprinkle coconut over the glaze. (This gives the church a wintry look, so if it is a warm-weather project, substitute sparkling sugar of your favorite color.)

Apply glaze to the yard—all exposed areas of the base—and sprinkle coconut and colored sugar over the glaze. Green sprinkles over coconut make very convincing "grass."

Chocolate Mint Fence

This rickety old fence is easily fashioned from thin mints. Cut each wafer in half lengthwise, and then cut off the top corners to form little points. Spread out the fence pieces on wax paper and keep them cool so they don't melt.

Trees and Tombstones

It's time to add the fence. Using a thick bead of icing, outline the area you want to fence in, and let it sit for a minute. Set the chocolate fence pieces into the icing one at a time, allowing them to list and lean the way an old fence does.

In order to stand the trees and tombstones in the yard, scrape away small areas of ground covering with your finger. Make thick beads of icing on the exposed base and allow to set partially. Place the trees and tombstones into the icing, propping them up until they harden, if necessary.

Put a small amount of icing on a red raspberry drop or gumdrop and place it on top of the steeple roof.

In a small bowl, add red food paste—a little at a time—to the remaining icing, mixing well until you reach a shade you like. Clean out the pastry bag or decorator and fill it with the red icing. Using a small tip, outline the doors, windows and steeple base (and anywhere else you see fit) to add a splash of color. You might even want to outline the tombstones. Your completed church and churchyard look stately—but just a little bit spooky.

Set mint fence pieces into a bead of icing, allowing them to list

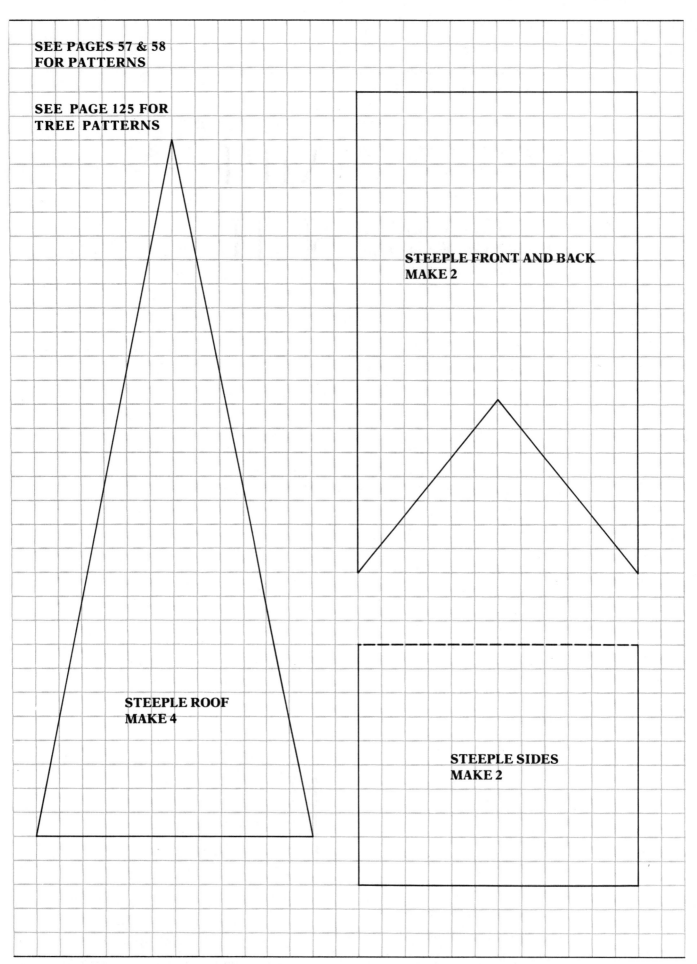

SEE PAGES 57 & 58
FOR PATTERNS

SEE PAGE 125 FOR
TREE PATTERNS

STEEPLE FRONT AND BACK
MAKE 2

STEEPLE ROOF
MAKE 4

STEEPLE SIDES
MAKE 2

9

SOUTHAMPTON VICTORIAN HOUSE

For splendor, nothing tops this gracious Queen Anne High Victorian house, with its intersecting roofs, wrap-around porch, arched windows and other fine detailing. One look reveals that this architectural style dates from an era when life—at least for some—was a long, relaxed and elegant affair, complete with croquet on the lawn and lots of time for reading and rocking on the front porch.

Building this lovely house in gingerbread takes some time and concentration, but the rewarding result is surely worth it. Just find a quiet afternoon and set to work.

This particular model includes a striking two-story bay window, dormer, and even a couple of those rocking chairs for the front porch. Trimming in two colors provides a bright, cheerful look, and flowers in the windows, along the border and around the front porch complete the springy, Southampton effect. This gingerbread creation makes a lovely gift or party centerpiece, particularly if you have friends with a passion for Victoriana.

Before beginning the Southampton Victorian, have the following ingredients and materials handy:

INGREDIENTS

Basic Gingerbread Dough: two batches will suffice for the house and lots of extra cookies (See p. 12.)

Icing: white for assembly (See p. 17.)

Food color or paste for mixing decorative icing

Glaze (See p. 20.)

Coconut

Green sprinkles

MATERIALS

Paper pattern pieces cut out and labeled (See p. 10.)

Base for structure, at least 14″ x 18″

String and scissors

Decorator or pastry bag

Brush for glaze

Mix and roll out your dough, cut out the paper pattern pieces and bake the gingerbread parts according to the basic instructions found on pp. 10-16. When all the house parts have been baked and cooled, along with any people, animal or other decorative cookies you decide you'll want to add later (see pp. 123-27), it's time to assemble the Victorian house.

ASSEMBLING THE HOUSE

Walls

Place the wall pieces, smooth side down, on a flat work space and make beads of icing along each of the vertical edges. Carefully decide on the placement of the house on its base, making sure to allow space for the side porch.

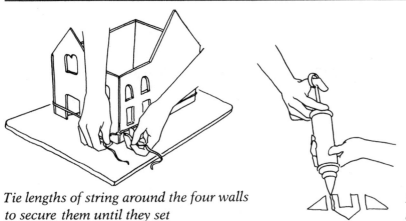

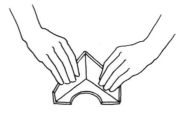

Stand the two front entry roof pieces against the gable piece, joining them at the peak

Tie lengths of string around the four walls to secure them until they set

Make a bead of icing between dormer pieces

(For this particular house, most of the color and detail will be on the house itself, rather than in the landscaping.)

Stand up the back end wall and the plain side wall—the one without the bay window—and attach them, propping them together until the icing is set. (If the icing is sufficiently stiff, this should only take a moment.) Attach the other side wall and finally the front wall in a similar manner. Tie two lengths of string around the walls at top and bottom to keep them secure until the icing has set hard. To reinforce the base, make a bead of icing along the groundline of the house, where it meets the base. Smooth any excess icing with your moistened finger, filling in any gaps that may have formed in the vertical wall joints.

Dormers

Place the three dormer pieces—the front and two sides—smooth side down, side by side. Make a bead of icing along the vertical edges of each piece where they will join, as you did the walls. To join them, leave the front piece flat on the work surface and stand up the two sides on top of it. Hold them in place until the icing begins to set and then prop if necessary.

Front Entry Roof

Place the three pieces for the front entry roof—the right and left roof sections and the gable end—side by side, smooth side down. Make beads of icing along the sides of the gable, along the sides of the roof pieces where they will meet the gable, and along the sides of the roof pieces that will form the peak. Stand the two roof pieces up on the gable piece, joining them at the peak. Prop if necessary until the icing has hardened.

Rockers

Each rocker has two sides and two square pieces, which form the back and seat. Place the two side pieces smooth side down and make dots of icing on their legs (just under the arm rests) and along the back frame. Stand up the seat piece in the dots on the legs and the back piece along the back frame. Hold carefully until the icing has set. Add more icing dots to the seat and back to hold the second side of the rocker. Then place the other side on top, lining it up with the first side piece—so that the finished rocker is straight. Allow it to harden fully. Make several, to be placed on the front porch of your house later.

Bay Window

Place the three pieces of the bay window—the front and two sides—smooth side down. Make a bead of icing along each vertical edge where the three pieces will meet. Then make an imaginary line down the side wall where the gable angle begins. Make a thick bead of icing $1/2''$ in from the imaginary line and $1/2''$ in from the back end of the side wall.

Stand up the two side pieces in the thick beads of icing. Angle the pieces in slightly. Hold them until they are firm enough to stand but are still adjustable.

Carefully put the bay window front in place, adjusting the angle of the two side pieces to fit. Make sure that the gable of the front piece lines up with the gable of the side wall. Smooth any excess icing along the joints and fill in any gaps. Finally, make a bead of icing along the groundline to secure the bay window to the base.

Porch Base

Put the porch base in place on your house base, $1/4''$ from the house (up against the icing bead along the base of the walls). Tack it with dots of icing along the house, and make a bead of icing along the front and side edges of the porch.

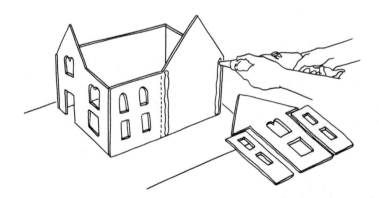

Run beads of icing down the side wall where the bay window will go

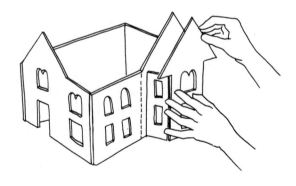

Carefully put the bay window front in place, adjusting the two side pieces to fit

Once the roof sides have been added, run a thin bead of icing along the peak and the roof side wall joints

Put the roof ends in place and hold them until the icing sets

Roof Side Pieces

Place the two roof side pieces smooth side down, leaving ⅛″ space between them. Make a thick bead of icing along the space and push the pieces together to form a joint. Then make a thick bead of icing along the top of the two side walls. Put the two roof pieces carefully in place. One side of the roof will butt up against the gable of the side wall. Ice along this joint between the roof and the gable of the side wall.

The other side of the roof must sit directly on the top edge of the side wall, and will need to be propped in place while the icing hardens.

Make a thin bead of icing along the peak and roof side wall joints to add stiffness and fill in any gaps. Smooth excess icing with a moistened finger and allow the roof to set fully before continuing.

Roof Ends

Make beads of icing along the exposed roof edges and the wall edges. Put the roof ends in place and hold them until the icing has set. Then make a thin bead of icing along the joint where the front end roof meets the front entry gable.

Bay Window Roof

Make a bead of icing along each side of the bay window ceiling piece and carefully put it in place across the top of the bay window side pieces. Place the two bay window roof pieces (right and left), smooth side down, side by side with ⅛″ space between them. Make a thick bead of icing along the space and push the pieces together, forming a joint which will be the roof peak.

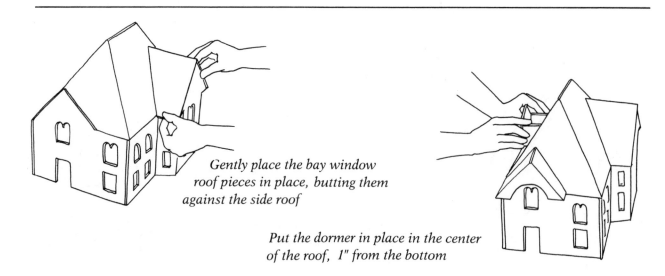

Gently place the bay window roof pieces in place, butting them against the side roof

Put the dormer in place in the center of the roof, 1" from the bottom

Make a bead of icing along the edges of the two gable pieces and the bay window ceiling piece. Put the two roof pieces in place, butting them up against the side roof. Hold them in place until the icing hardens.

Make a bead of icing on each side where the bay window roof meets the side roof. Smooth any excess.

Front Entry Roof

Make a bead of icing along the gable edge of the front entry and along the slanted edges of the front entry roof pieces where they will meet the front end roof.

Put the entry roof and gable in place, butting the roof pieces against the front end roof. Hold these for a moment until they set. Make beads of icing on both sides where the entry roof meets the front end roof.

Dormer

Measure the length of the side roof to find its center line. Measure up 1" from the bottom of the roof and make a bead of icing along the bottom edge of the front dormer piece and the two slanted edges of the side pieces where they will meet the side roof.

Put the dormer in place in the center of the roof, 1" from the bottom. Tie a length of string around the dormer and the rest of the house to hold the dormer while the icing hardens.

Dormer Roof

Place the two pieces (right and left) side by side, smooth side up, with ⅛" space between them. Make a bead of icing along the space and push the pieces together to form a joint.

Make a bead of icing along the gable end and along the top edges of the side walls of the dormer. Put the roof pieces in place carefully. Make a bead of icing along the two slanted edges where the dormer roof joins the side roof and smooth any excess icing.

Front Door

Make a bead of icing along the two vertical edges of the door opening and stand up the doors—half open—smooth side out.

Porch

Make icing beads along the center of five of the porch post pieces; set the other five on top, forming double-thickness posts, and allow them to set for a moment.

Make mounds of icing for the porch posts to stand in and allow the icing mounds to set partially. Then stand up the posts in the icing, propping them if necessary.

Make a bead of icing along the front and side walls under the second-story windows, where the porch roof will meet them. Also make a bead of icing along the side of the bay window from under the second-story window to the top of the first-story window. Finally, make a bead on the top of each of the five posts.

Place the two porch roof pieces at right angles, smooth side up with the pieces touching at the front corner. Make a bead of icing along the two edges and push the pieces together to form a joint. The pieces will now form an angle to wrap around the house.

Carefully put the porch roof pieces in place on the posts, butting them up against the front and side walls and the side wall of the bay window.

Hold the roof gently in place for a moment. Smooth the icing along the joint between the porch roof and the house wall.

Believe it or not, you're finished with the construction! Now that the hard part is behind you, take a break and admire your work. Begin thinking about decoration.

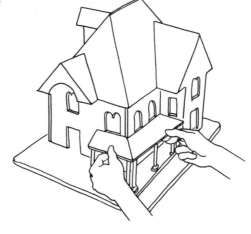

Place the two porch roof pieces
in place on the posts

DECORATION

Divide the remaining icing into two small bowls. Add food color or paste gradually, first making one bowl of icing bright pink and then making the other bowl bright green.

Clean your pastry bag or decorator. (Remember, you'll have to clean it whenever you change colors, so plan carefully and finish with one color before you begin using the other. Don't forget to decorate your cookies as you go along.)

Brush glaze on all the roof surfaces and sprinkle them generously with coconut for texture, eye-appeal—and flavor. Then glaze the base around the house and sprinkle it first with coconut, then with green sprinkles.

Fit your decorator with a plain, thin tip and fill it with green icing. Carefully edge the doors and arched windows. Draw an arch on the front of the bay window above the actual cut-out windows.

Change to a wide, swirly decorating tip and make a border of green "foliage" around the edge of the house at its base.

Clean your decorator and fill it with the pink icing. (Leave the swirly tip in place.) Make decorative beads along the roof peaks, with little pinnacles at the ends. Make a pink bead along the porch roof/wall joint. Along the porch, make swirly mounds of pink flowers.

Make pink beads along the bottom edges of the windows, for a "window box" look. Finally, make a border of pink flowers around the edge of the base, on top of the green foliage, completing your "garden."

If you have made and decorated any shrubbery, people or animal cookies to populate your Victorian house, now is the time to place them around the completed house. In order to stand them up, scrape away patches of the ground cover and make thick beads of icing. Stand the cookies in the icing and hold or prop them until they've set.

Your elaborate handiwork is complete! Have a cookie and just wait for the astonished expressions of your family and friends. In spite of its weight and intricacy, your house will be quite sturdy and portable when it's fully set.

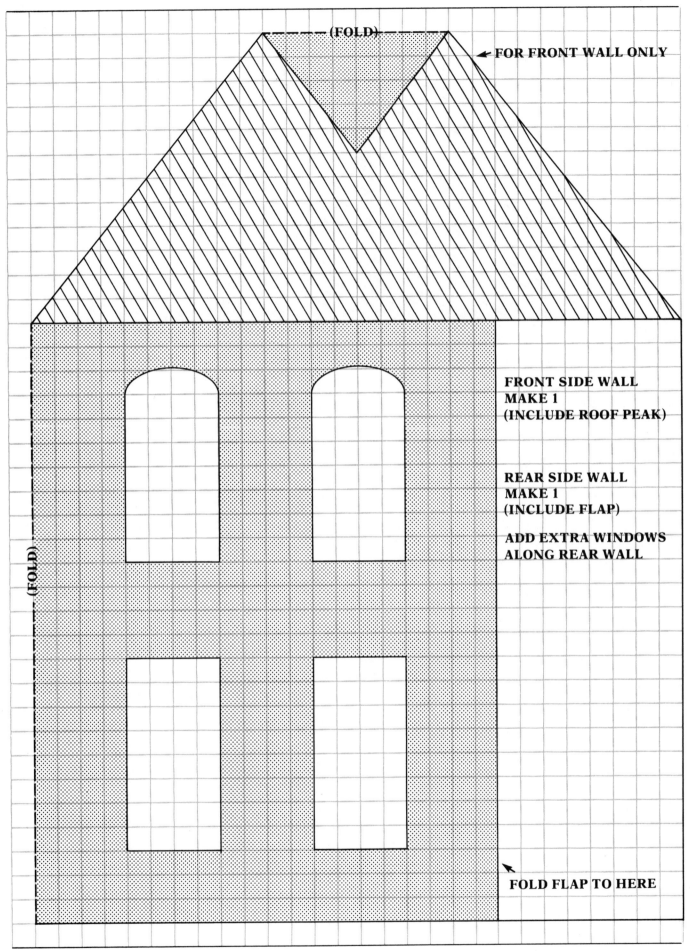

(FOLD)

FOR FRONT WALL ONLY

(FOLD)

**FRONT SIDE WALL
MAKE 1
(INCLUDE ROOF PEAK)**

**REAR SIDE WALL
MAKE 1
(INCLUDE FLAP)**

**ADD EXTRA WINDOWS
ALONG REAR WALL**

FOLD FLAP TO HERE

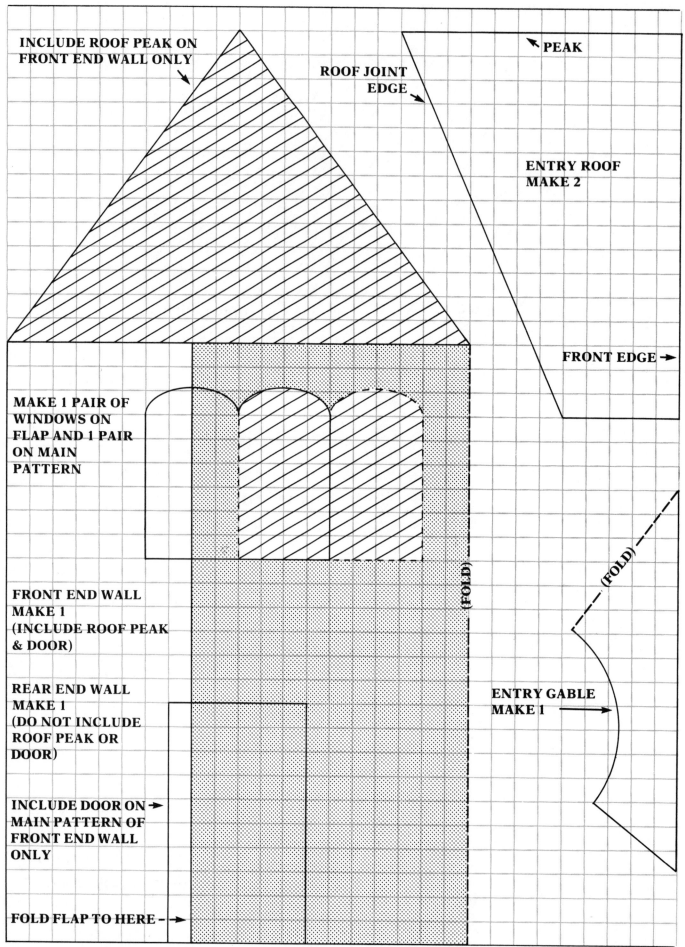

INCLUDE ROOF PEAK ON
FRONT END WALL ONLY

PEAK

ROOF JOINT
EDGE

ENTRY ROOF
MAKE 2

FRONT EDGE →

MAKE 1 PAIR OF
WINDOWS ON
FLAP AND 1 PAIR
ON MAIN
PATTERN

(FOLD)

(FOLD)

FRONT END WALL
MAKE 1
(INCLUDE ROOF PEAK
& DOOR)

REAR END WALL
MAKE 1
(DO NOT INCLUDE
ROOF PEAK OR
DOOR)

ENTRY GABLE
MAKE 1 →

INCLUDE DOOR ON →
MAIN PATTERN OF
FRONT END WALL
ONLY

FOLD FLAP TO HERE - →

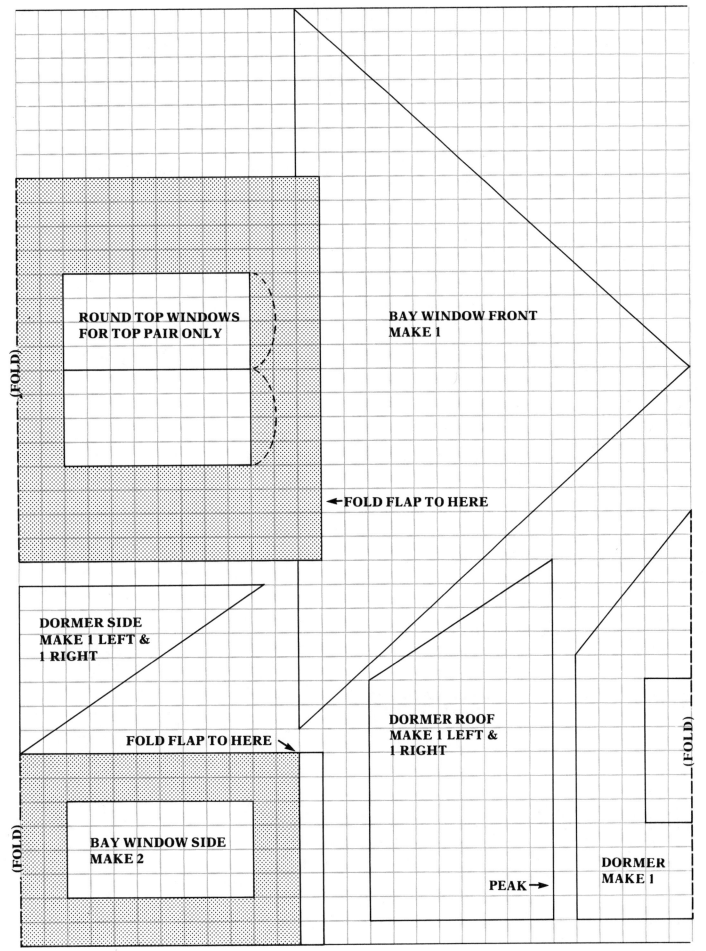

ROUND TOP WINDOWS
FOR TOP PAIR ONLY

(FOLD)

BAY WINDOW FRONT
MAKE 1

←FOLD FLAP TO HERE

DORMER SIDE
MAKE 1 LEFT &
1 RIGHT

DORMER ROOF
MAKE 1 LEFT &
1 RIGHT

FOLD FLAP TO HERE →

(FOLD)

BAY WINDOW SIDE
MAKE 2

(FOLD)

PEAK →

DORMER
MAKE 1

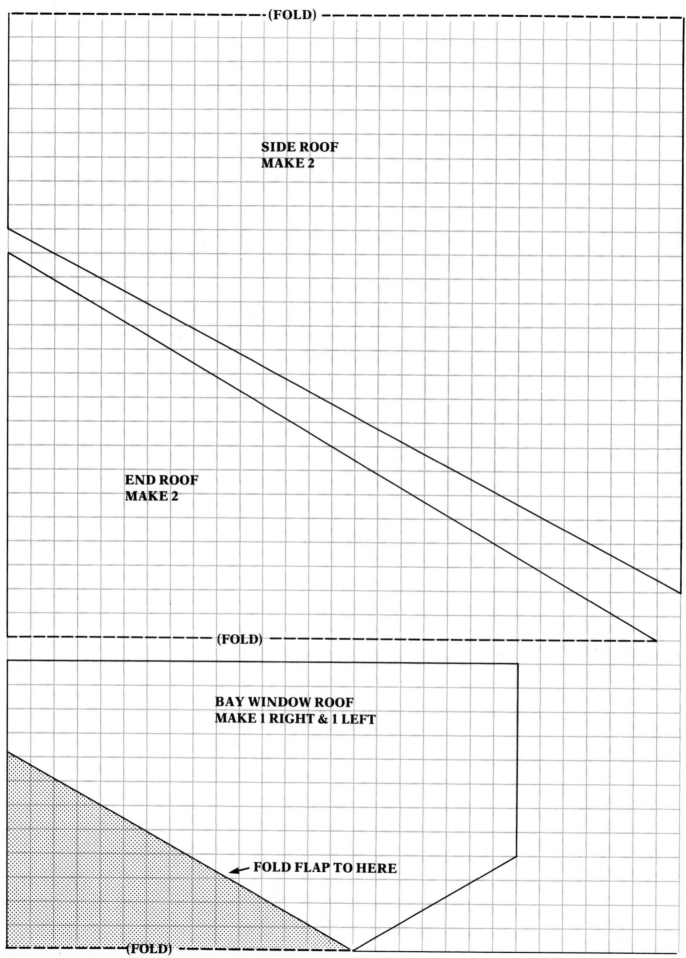

SIDE ROOF
MAKE 2

END ROOF
MAKE 2

(FOLD)

(FOLD)

BAY WINDOW ROOF
MAKE 1 RIGHT & 1 LEFT

← FOLD FLAP TO HERE

(FOLD)

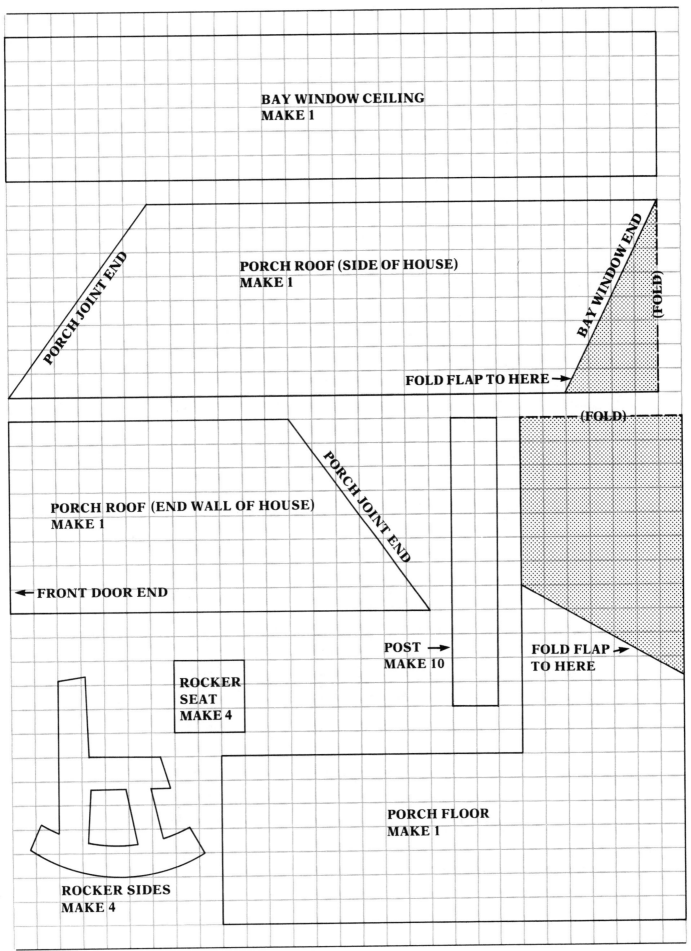

BAY WINDOW CEILING
MAKE 1

PORCH JOINT END

PORCH ROOF (SIDE OF HOUSE)
MAKE 1

BAY WINDOW END

(FOLD)

FOLD FLAP TO HERE

(FOLD)

PORCH ROOF (END WALL OF HOUSE)
MAKE 1

PORCH JOINT END

← FRONT DOOR END

FOLD FLAP →
TO HERE

POST →
MAKE 10

ROCKER
SEAT
MAKE 4

PORCH FLOOR
MAKE 1

ROCKER SIDES
MAKE 4

10

SKYSCRAPER AND TOWNHOUSE

Sprawling country houses are nice, but city-dwellers are entitled to gingerbread treats in their neighborhood's image, too. Here is a tasty cityscape, perfect for apartment-warmings or any urban celebration.

The townhouse and skyscraper are very easy to build—they're just stacked boxes, really. The fun is in adding details like icing and candy trim, steps, shrubbery, sidewalks, lampposts, even a fire hydrant for Spot. Then add a few cars parked at the curb and your urban landscape is complete.

Before you begin building your townhouse and skyscraper, have the following ingredients and materials ready:

INGREDIENTS

Chocolate Cookie Dough: two
  batches (See p. 13.)
Icing: white for assembly (See p. 17.)
Red and yellow food color or
  paste for decorative icing

Glaze (See p. 20.)
Large round gumdrops, large
  raspberry drops, sunflower
  seeds, small disc candies,
  M & M's or Reese's Pieces

MATERIALS

Pattern pieces for the buildings as
  well as bushes, trees and steps,
  cut out and labeled (See p. 10.)
Base, at least 14" x 18"

Cake decorator or pastry bag
Brush for glaze
Plastic straws for lampposts
Skewer to etch design

Mix and roll out your dough, cut out the paper pattern pieces and bake the gingerbread parts according to the basic instructions found on pp. 10-16. As in the train project, it is a good idea to do some decorating of the cookie pieces before you begin assembling the buildings. So wait until all of the gingerbread has cooled thoroughly and begin. Remember that you'll always be decorating the smooth "outsides" of the cookies, and that you must let the icing harden fully before assembling the structures. Decorate the car cookies as well, so they'll have time to dry before you assemble and "park" them.

PRE-ASSEMBLY DECORATION

Divide the icing in half, saving one half in a covered bowl for later use in assembly. Divide the other half in half again, so you have two small batches. Mix one small batch with yellow food color or paste, and the other with red, adding the color slowly until you mix shades that you like.

Place a thin, plain tip on your decorator and fill it with the red icing. Make decorative beads in the shape of windows and doors on the pieces for both buildings. Outline the bushes and the silhouettes of the cars. Draw the

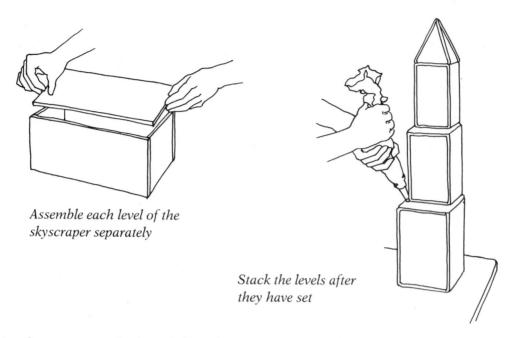

Assemble each level of the skyscraper separately

Stack the levels after they have set

roof pattern on the spire of the skyscraper and some cornice trim on the townhouse.

Clean the decorator (when you're sure that you've applied all the red trim you want), and fill it with yellow icing. Using the thin, plain tip again, draw quoins on the corners of the townhouse. Make beads of icing along the edges of the stair pieces. Add some yellow to the bushes, cars and clock.

Allow time for the icing to harden, and then begin to assemble the buildings.

ASSEMBLY

Before you begin, clean the decorator again, and fill it with the white icing you've been saving for assembly. Fit it with a medium tip this time.

Place the four walls of the townhouse smooth side down on the work surface. Make an even bead of icing along the four edges of the two side walls, where they will join the end walls. Decide where on the base you want to place the townhouse, and then stand one end and one side wall up together, forming a joint. Hold them for a minute while they set. Then stand the second side wall up, joining the other two walls, and finally, add the remaining end wall. Tie two strings around the walls, one at the base and one near the top. Make a bead of icing along the base of the townhouse to secure it to the base.

Follow the very same procedure to build three separate skyscraper stories, allowing them to set before stacking them. (Secure only the bottom level of the skyscraper to the base at first.) When the three stories have set sufficiently, make beads of icing along the exposed edges of the bottom and middle stories and set the roof pieces in place. While they set, you can build the skyscraper spire. Before the pieces are assembled, etch the roof design onto the smooth sides of the spire with a skewer.

Place the four pieces smooth side down on the table. Make beads of icing along the right-hand edge of each triangle. Assemble the four pieces, each overlapping the next, so as to keep the base square. Hold the pieces together with the flat edge resting on the table. Let the spire set.

By now, the walls of the three stories should be hardened in place. Make a bead of icing along the base of the middle story and set it in the center of the first story. Make a bead of icing along the joint where the two levels meet. Now make a bead of icing along the base edge of the top story. Set it in the center of the middle story. Make a bead of icing where the joints meet. Let this set for 10 minutes or so. Then make a bead of icing along the base of the spire and set it on top of the third story.

Both of your buildings are standing now! Take a moment to admire your own handiwork, and plan all the frills to come.

Streetlights

Place two round gumdrops on top of each other, and stick a larger gumdrop or a raspberry drop in the center of them. Stick a plastic straw into the gumdrop and then stick yet another gumdrop atop the straw.

Fire Hydrant

Stack three large round gumdrops on top of one another and crown them with a red gumdrop or raspberry drop.

Stairs

Stairs are best assembled on their sides. With the smooth sides facing the table, make a bead of icing along the side railing where the bottom and back piece will sit. Also make a bead along the lower back edge of the stairs, where the bottom will join. Make beads of icing along the sides and fronts of the four steps, and set them in place. Let the stair structure set, and then ice along the exposed edge and put the other side piece in place.

Assemble stairs on their sides

Make beads of icing along the sides and fronts of the steps

DECORATION

When the buildings are all assembled, clean your decorator and switch back to the yellow icing. Fit the decorator with a fluted tip, and make decorative beads along the wall joints of the skyscraper and along the edges of each roof—including the spire. Set a raspberry drop on top of the spire, and set candies into the icing.

Cut gumdrop rings in half and stack them on the roofs, forming an art-deco pattern. Use two dabs of icing on each one to secure them.

Make decorative trim along the top of the townhouse roof. You can form dentils by spacing dabs of yellow icing along the red cornice lines under the roof eaves.

Make beads of icing along the wall joints if you wish, using a thinner fluted tip if you have one.

Cover the roof of the townhouse with M & M's or Reese's Pieces.

Set the bushes in mounds of icing, propping them until they are set. Add some candies for flowers around the shrubbery.

To make sidewalks or paths leading up to the doors of each building, glaze the path surface with a brush and then sprinkle with pastel candies. Use additional candies to form an edging or curb, placing them very carefully in rows. Fill in any bare surfaces with sunflower seeds, making sure to glaze first so they will stick.

Now set the lampposts and fire hydrants in place where you want them. If you've made any people or animal cookies, now is the time to set them in place. To do this, scrape away a bit of the ground cover and make a dab of icing in the space. Stand the cookie in the icing, propping or holding it until it sets.

In the same manner, place a few cars at the curb, just outside the lampposts. Make a border of yellow icing around the edge of the base and fill in any bare spots with more sunflower seeds.

Your cityscape is complete—just add street noises.

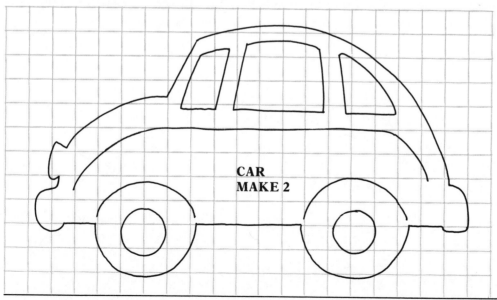

CAR
MAKE 2

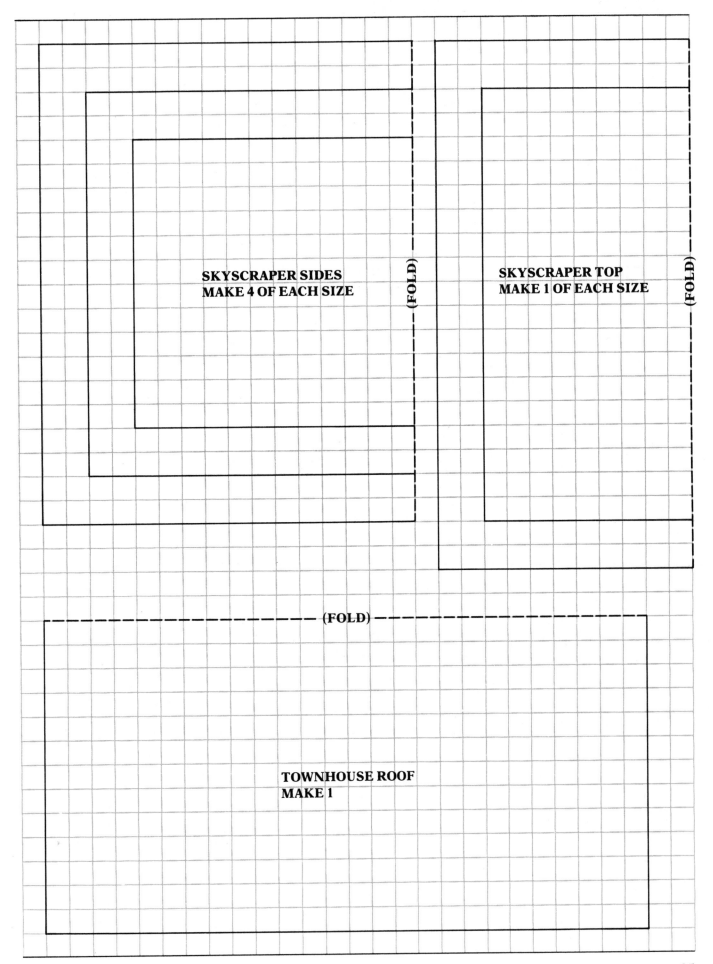

SKYSCRAPER SIDES
MAKE 4 OF EACH SIZE

(FOLD)

SKYSCRAPER TOP
MAKE 1 OF EACH SIZE

(FOLD)

(FOLD)

TOWNHOUSE ROOF
MAKE 1

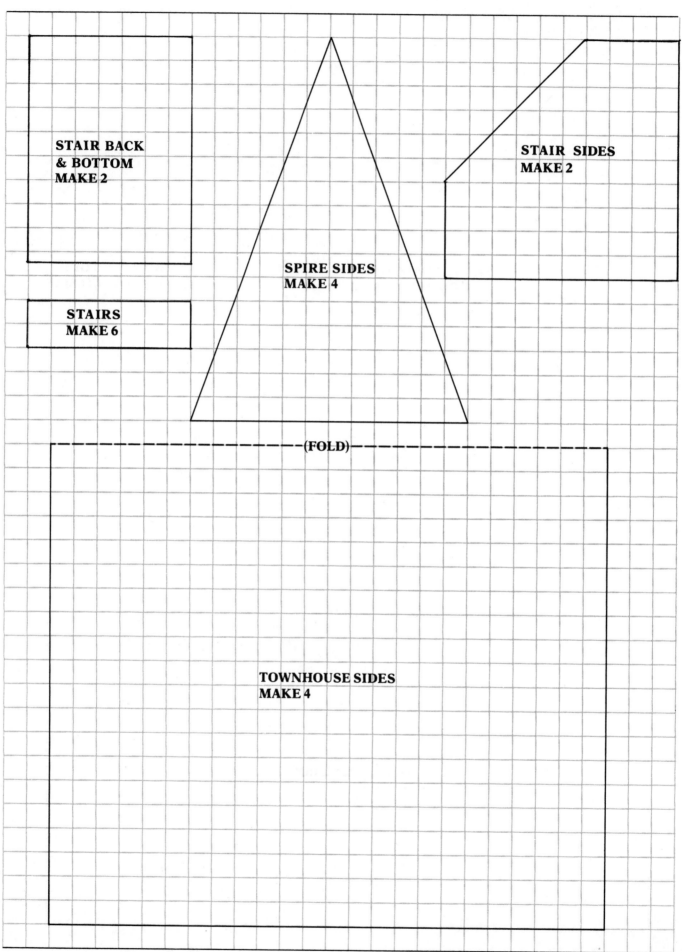

STAIR BACK
& BOTTOM
MAKE 2

STAIR SIDES
MAKE 2

STAIRS
MAKE 6

SPIRE SIDES
MAKE 4

(FOLD)

TOWNHOUSE SIDES
MAKE 4

11

BARN

The farm plan pictured here features a barn with a gambrel-style roof, which was popular in New England for houses as well as barns from around 1800 to 1860. All that space under the big roof was used for storing lots of hay. This is a perfect springtime project since it features lots of animals.

The icing decorations for this gingerbread model should be kept fairly simple without too many colors. (The big barn shape, the fence, and loads of animals provide all the decoration it needs.) Just the plain white icing with some bright red trim is most effective.

Have the following ingredients and materials ready before you start the farm:

INGREDIENTS

Basic Gingerbread Dough: one batch to make the barn and the fence (See p. 12.)

Chocolate Cookie Dough: one batch for all the animal cookies (You can substitute any of the recipes, so just decide what flavor and color you want the animals to be. See p. 13.)

Red licorice

Mini-chocolate chips for decoration

Ground nuts

Oatmeal for barnyard texture

Glaze (See p. 20.)

Icing: one batch (See p. 17.)

Red food color or paste

MATERIALS

Paper patterns cut out and labeled (See p. 10.)

Very large base for barnyard setting: at least 16″ x 20″

Brush for glaze

Cake decorator or pastry bag with assorted tips

String

Mix and roll out your dough, cut out the paper pattern pieces and bake the gingerbread parts according to the basic instructions found on pp. 10-16. After you have prepared all the pattern pieces and baked the barn parts in gingerbread, you're ready to start assembling it. You should also have made at least a dozen animal cookies to be used in decorating.

ASSEMBLING THE BARN

Walls

Begin by icing the joints for the four walls. Make a bead of icing on the vertical edges of the two side walls. Start with the back side wall and the back end wall and place them in one corner of the base. Using a corner of the base helps to keep the barn straight and square. Then raise the front side wall joining it to the rear end wall. Finally, the front end wall with the door opening goes up to complete the shape. Tie two lengths of string around the walls at the top and base. Secure the barn to the base with a bead of icing at the bottom. Another bead of icing along the base on the inside is helpful, but not essential. Smooth the icing of the outside corner joints with your finger, filling in any spaces.

Upper Roof

A gambrel roof has four pieces—two for the top and two for the sides. Place the two top roof pieces side by side, smooth sides up, with 1/8" space between them. Join the longest sides on each of these pieces together to make the roof peak; they overhang where they join the roof sides. Make an icing bead along the 1/8" space between the pieces. Also make icing beads along the top edges of the two end walls. Do not ice the lower half of the end walls or the top edges of the side walls yet. That will be done when you put on the lower half of the roof.

Join the two top pieces together and place on top of the walls. Hold them together for a minute or so until the icing sets a bit. Then tie a length of string around each side of the roof where it overhangs. While this top part of the roof is setting (about 15 minutes), you can do some decorating around the windows or door, or you could always make some more cookies. Untie the strings from around the top and the bottom of the walls and remove them. (Leave the strings in place around the upper roof.) Make a decorative bead of icing around the door, window openings, and along the four wall joints. The back side and back end of the barn should be decorated with vertical lines of icing to simulate vertical barn boards. Decorate the barn door pieces with icing and place at angles from the door opening.

Carefully set the upper roof in place

Tie lengths of string around the overhanging ends of the upper roof

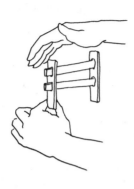 

Carefully slip the fence rails into place

Carefully set the lower roof pieces in place and hold them for a minute

Fence

What's a barn without a rail fence around it to keep the animals from wandering? The fence does take some patience to make but the effect is well worth the effort.

Space the fence posts on the base so that the rails extend about ¹/₂″ on either side. The poles must be turned sideways so that the rails can go through the holes you made when cutting out the cookie pieces. Make a mound of icing for each pole. When partially hardened, stand the pole in it and prop up if necessary. Allow the icing to harden further before adding the rails, then carefully slip them into place. Add a bit more icing if any of the poles seem wobbly. The corners require two posts so that each rail can go through a hole.

Lower Roof

Untie the strings from around the upper roof ends. Make a bead of icing along the lower edges of the top roof pieces which are already in place, down the rest of the end wall edges, and along the top edges of the side walls. Make another bead along the top edge of each side of the two lower roof pieces. Fit the lower roof pieces into place one at a time. Hold each piece in place for a minute, then tie lengths of string around the roof ends—both upper and lower.

Animals and Decorations

By now the roof is on and the fence should be up. Make mounds of icing where you want to place animal cookies—decorate them first if you want. They can be glazed and sprinkled with ground nuts, candy, sugar or coconut. Features can be added with colored icing, but try not to over-decorate.

The charm here is in the simplicity of all the many animal shapes. Place the animals in the mounds of half-hardened icing.

Make a decorative bead of icing along the outside of the base—around the fence.

Brush the glaze evenly onto the surface of the barnyard base and sprinkle with oatmeal for texture.

Untie the strings on the roof. Make a thin decorative bead of icing along the roof joints. Carefully place mini-chocolate chips in a row along the joints, or place strips of red licorice along them. You can also glaze and sprinkle the roof with nuts, oatmeal, coconuts, or candy if you like.

Decorate the barn with colored icing

Carefully place mini-chocolate chips along the roof peaks

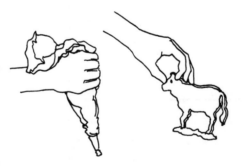

Stand animal cookies into mounds of half-hardened icing

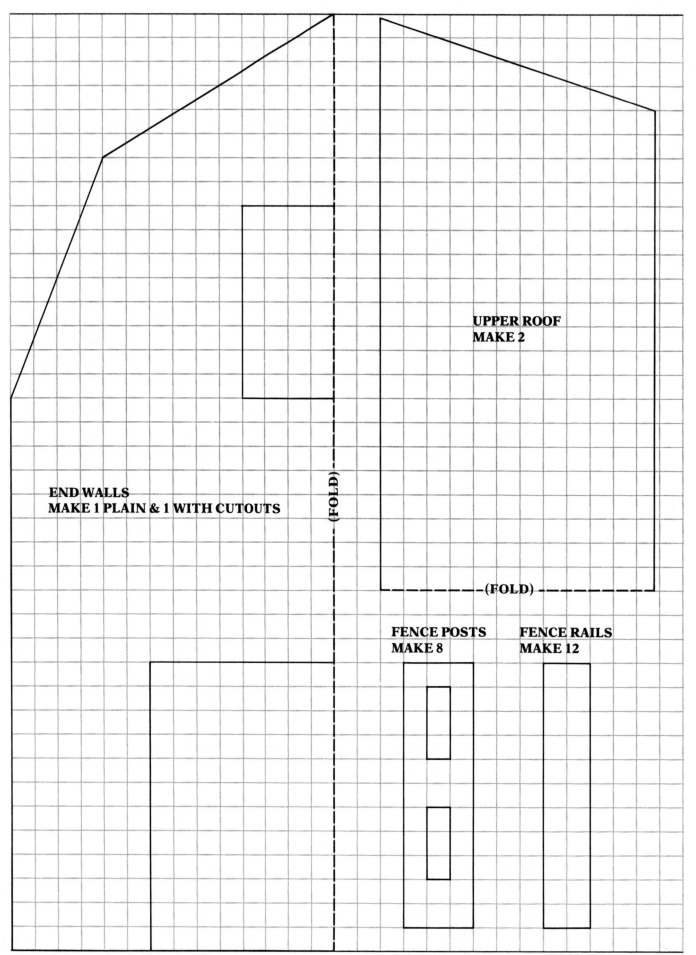

**UPPER ROOF
MAKE 2**

**END WALLS
MAKE 1 PLAIN & 1 WITH CUTOUTS**

(FOLD)

(FOLD)

**FENCE POSTS
MAKE 8**

**FENCE RAILS
MAKE 12**

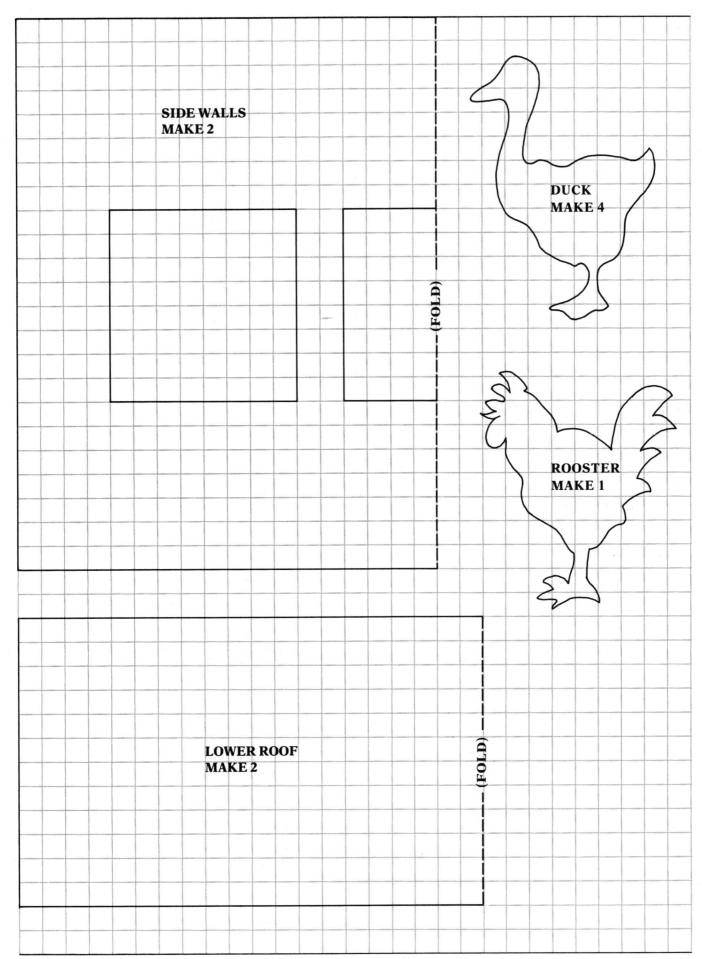

**SIDE WALLS
MAKE 2**

(FOLD)

**DUCK
MAKE 4**

**ROOSTER
MAKE 1**

**LOWER ROOF
MAKE 2**

(FOLD)

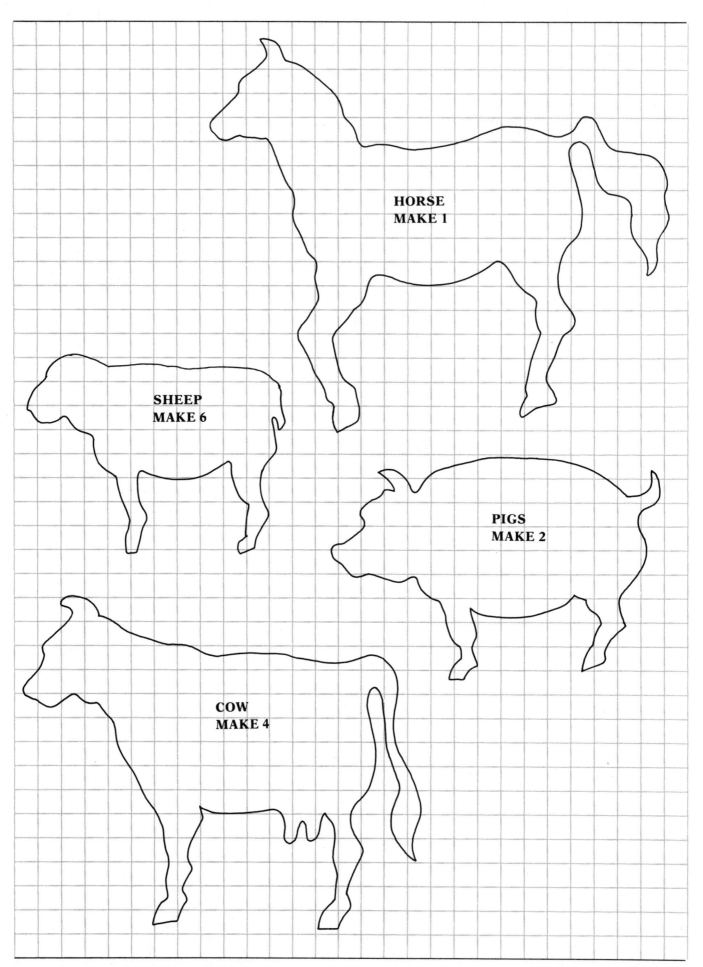

HORSE
MAKE 1

SHEEP
MAKE 6

PIGS
MAKE 2

COW
MAKE 4

12

ARK

When your children begin to feel as if it will never stop raining outside, it's the perfect time to build an ark—out of gingerbread, that is. This absorbing rainy-day project will also make a lively party decoration that's delicious to eat, especially with all the pairs of animal cookies marching up the gangplank and lounging on the deck. Round up your junior Noahs, and set to work!

Before you begin to construct your ark, be sure and have the following ingredients and materials handy:

INGREDIENTS

Chocolate Cookie Dough: one
   batch (See p. 13.)
Vanilla Cookie Dough: one batch
   (See p. 13.)
Icing: white for assembly
   (See p. 17.)

Yellow food color or paste, to
   make decorative icing
Glaze (See p. 20.)
Candy decoration: circular
   gumdrops, small disc candies,
   coconut

MATERIALS

Pattern pieces, cut out and
   labeled (See p. 10.)
Base, at least 14" x 16"
Cake decorator or pastry bag,
   with small and medium tips

Brush for glaze
Plastic straw, matte knife and
   paper for flag
String

Mix and roll out your dough, cut out the paper pattern pieces and bake the gingerbread parts according to the basic instructions found on pp. 10-16. After you've baked and cooled all of the ark parts—and lots of cookie animals (be sure and bake a right and left of each animal, so you'll have pairs)—you are ready to begin boat-building.

ARK ASSEMBLY

The ark is constructed in three separate "decks." All the decks are assembled upside down.

Place all the pieces for the lowest deck smooth side down on the table. Fill your decorator with white icing and fit it with a medium tip. Make a bead of icing along the four edges of the roof piece, and along the edges of the side pieces where they will meet the end pieces. Stand the four walls, angling them in so that they fit together. Then make a bead of icing along the outside where the joints meet. Prop your structure with small spice jars from the inside, until the walls are set. Then remove the jars.

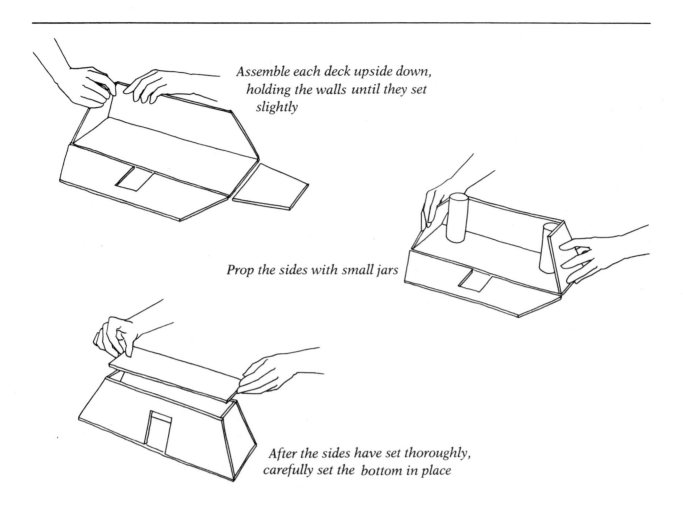

Assemble each deck upside down, holding the walls until they set slightly

Prop the sides with small jars

After the sides have set thoroughly, carefully set the bottom in place

Make a bead of icing along the exposed edges of the four walls and place the bottom piece in place. Let the whole thing set for at least 10 minutes before turning it upright.

The middle and upper decks are constructed in just the same way, in an upside down position. Lay the five pieces of the middle deck on the table, smooth side down. Make a bead of icing along the four edges of the top (which is your base for construction purposes), and along the edges of the side pieces where they will meet the end pieces. Stand the side and end pieces in place. Use small jars to prop the walls, and let the pieces set.

Repeat the procedure for the top deck, making sure that the hole has been cut in the roof part, where the flag will later be mounted.

Be sure all three decks have thoroughly set before setting them in place one on top of another.

To erect the ark, carefully place the lower deck in the center of the back edge of your base, making sure it's in the upright position. Secure the ark to the base with a bead of icing along the bottom.

With the middle and top decks still in the upside down position, make beads of icing along their exposed edges. Set the middle deck upright in the center of the lower deck. Then set the upper deck (or "wheelhouse") in place in the center of the middle deck. Let the three decks harden.

Gently set the ramp in place against the ark. You've built a boat!

ANIMAL DECORATION

Before the animals take their place on board, you'll want to add some decorative details. Clean your decorator and fit it with the small tip. Place the white icing you have left in a small bowl and gradually mix in yellow food color or paste until you've created a shade you like. Fill your decorator with yellow icing.

Make thin beads of icing around the edges of the cookies (remembering always to decorate the smooth sides only). Add other details, such as eyes, mane on the lions, spots and stripes—and don't forget to decorate Noah's beard. Let the icing harden before attaching the animal pairs.

Pairing the Animals

So they won't wander off and get separated, each of the animal pairs is joined with a spreader. These pairs are most easily constructed on their sides.

Carefully, so as not to crack the icing decorations, place one animal with the icing facing the table. Make beads of icing along the outer edge of one of the spreaders and set it in place against the animal. Hold briefly until the icing has set. Repeat this procedure for one animal of each pair, so that the spreaders can set thoroughly before you add the second animal. (This should take only around five minutes.)

Make a bead of icing along the exposed edges of the spreaders and carefully set the other animals in place, making sure both are facing the same direction. The decorated sides should be facing out, of course. Leave them on their sides for a few minutes while they set.

While the animals are setting, decorate the ark.

DECORATING THE ARK

With the thin tip on your decorator, draw portholes on the side of your boat. Make beads of icing along the decks and set the small round mints in place. Add your favorite candies wherever you'd like, attaching them with dabs of

Carefully set the second animal in place

icing, or piling them on the decks loosely so the animals will have plenty of provisions for their journey.

Make a thick bead of icing along the outer edge of the base and set large, round gumdrops into it.

Now the ark is complete, and all that's left is to add the passengers. Arrange Noah and his parade of animals around the ark and make dabs of icing to secure them. Set Noah up by the wheelhouse in a mound of icing so he can watch over his menagerie.

Attach the paper flag to the plastic straws by making a 2″ slit in the straw and slipping the flag in place. Set the flag into the top of the wheelhouse.

Brush glaze on the base wherever it is uncovered, and sprinkle coconut generously over its surface.

Now, let it rain! Noah and his vessel have smooth sailing ahead—until they encounter your hungry guests.

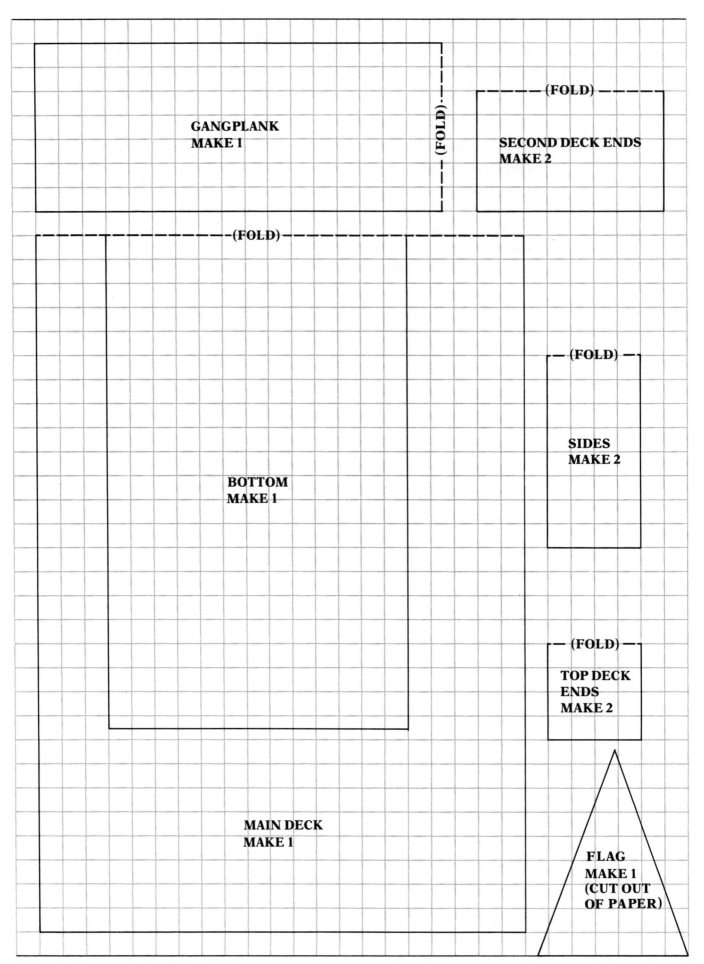

GANGPLANK
MAKE 1

(FOLD)

(FOLD)

SECOND DECK ENDS
MAKE 2

(FOLD)

BOTTOM
MAKE 1

SIDES
MAKE 2

(FOLD)

TOP DECK
ENDS
MAKE 2

MAIN DECK
MAKE 1

FLAG
MAKE 1
(CUT OUT
OF PAPER)

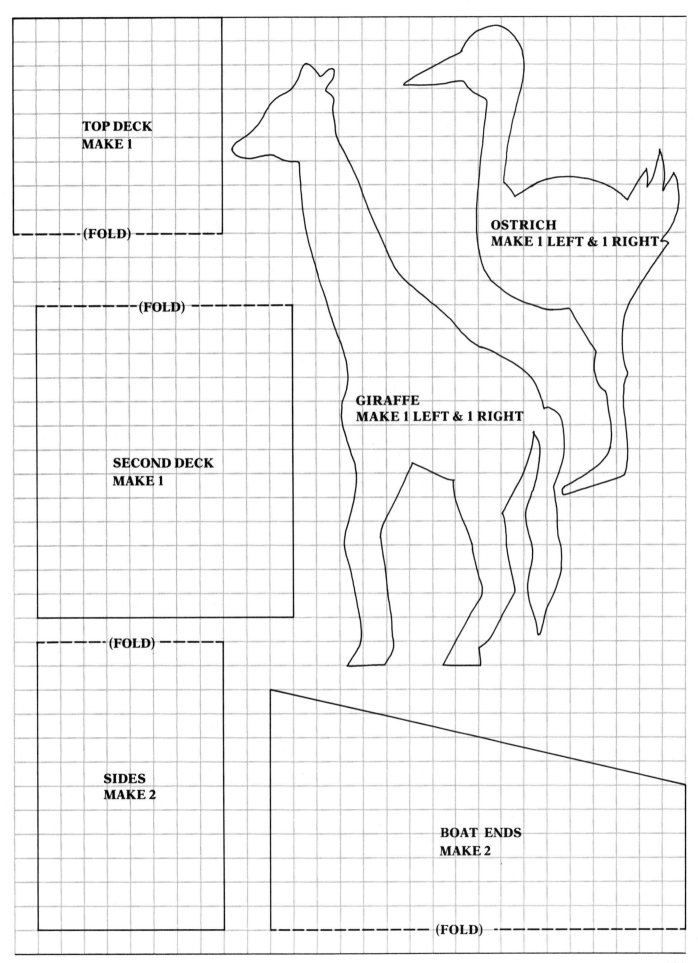

TOP DECK MAKE 1

— — (FOLD) — —

— — (FOLD) — — —

SECOND DECK MAKE 1

— — (FOLD) — — —

SIDES MAKE 2

GIRAFFE MAKE 1 LEFT & 1 RIGHT

OSTRICH MAKE 1 LEFT & 1 RIGHT

BOAT ENDS MAKE 2

— — — — — (FOLD) — — — — —

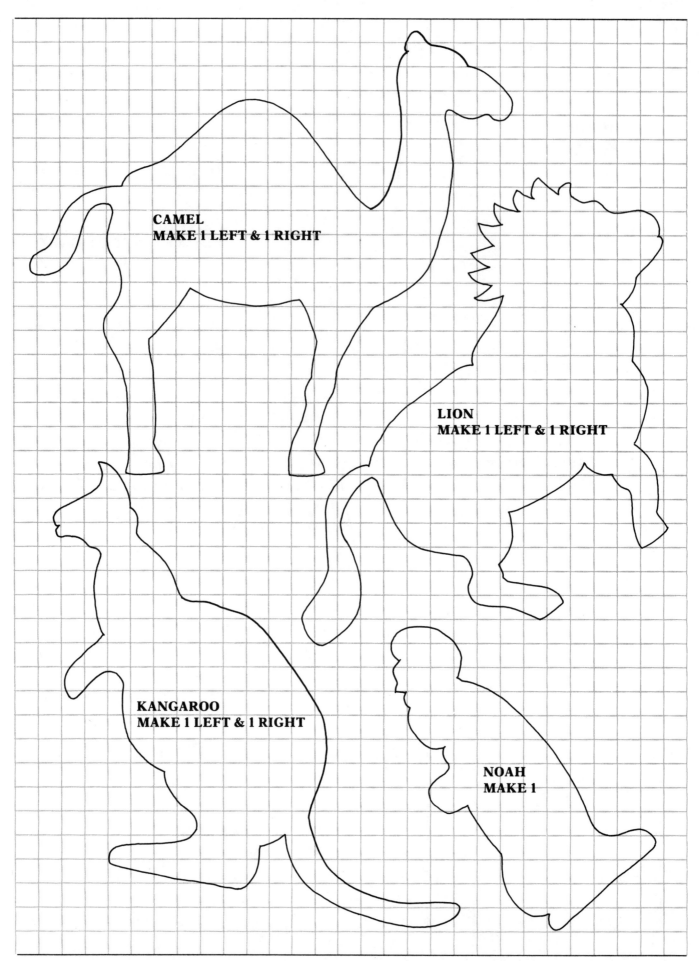

CAMEL
MAKE 1 LEFT & 1 RIGHT

LION
MAKE 1 LEFT & 1 RIGHT

KANGAROO
MAKE 1 LEFT & 1 RIGHT

NOAH
MAKE 1

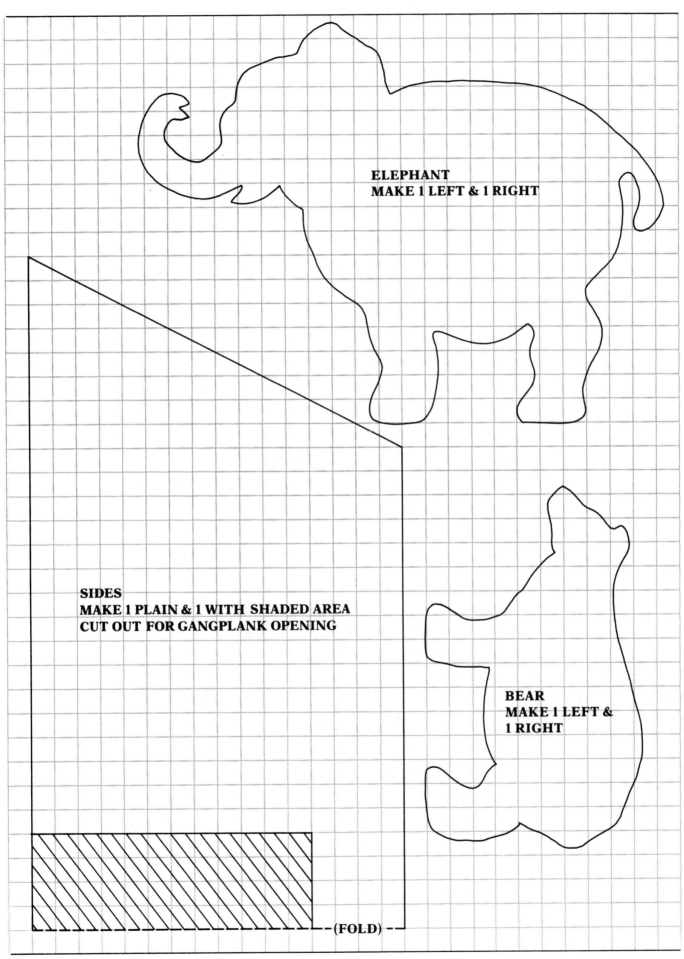

ELEPHANT
MAKE 1 LEFT & 1 RIGHT

SIDES
MAKE 1 PLAIN & 1 WITH SHADED AREA
CUT OUT FOR GANGPLANK OPENING

BEAR
MAKE 1 LEFT &
1 RIGHT

(FOLD)

13

TRAIN

All aboard! If you're searching for the perfect centerpiece for your child's birthday party, or would simply like a novel addition to any celebration, you're on the right track with this creation. It's a gingerbread train, pulled by a locomotive (complete with cowcatcher and smokestack), drawing a coal car, three box cars brimming with scrumptious sweets, and of course, a caboose!

This project is ideal for a group: the whole family, a slumber party or scout troop, or just the kids trapped inside on a rainy day. There's plenty of work for everyone to do something. So climb on board the Gingerbread Express. . . .

Before beginning construction, have the following materials and ingredients handy:

INGREDIENTS

Vanilla Cookie Dough: one batch
    (See p. 13.)
Chocolate Cookie Dough: one
    batch (See p. 13.)
Icing: white for assembly (See p. 17.)
Red food color or paste to make
    decorative icing

Candies, cookies, ice cream or
    other treats to fill the finished
    box cars (Chocolate kisses,
    mints, red hots and nonpareils
    are attractive)

MATERIALS

Pattern pieces, cut out and
    labeled (See p. 10.)

Base, at least 14″ x 18″
Cake decorator or pastry bag

Mix and roll out your dough, cut out the paper pattern pieces and bake the gingerbread parts according to the basic instructions found on pp. 10-16. Once you've baked and fully cooled the pieces (half in chocolate dough, half in vanilla, so you can have different-colored train cars), you're ready to do some pre-assembly decorating. As in the Santa and Sled project, it is simpler to decorate the train pieces before they are assembled.

Divide the icing into a large and a small batch, and set the large batch aside—covered so it won't harden—for later assembly. Mix red food paste into the smaller batch until you reach a shade you like.

Fill the decorator with the red icing and attach a small tip. Carefully outline each car in red. Make a red border around each wheel and draw red spokes. If you wish to write a holiday or birthday message on the sides of the cars, this is the best time to do it, keeping in mind the order and direction that the cars will be in when assembled. (All through decoration, remember to ice the smooth outsides of the cookies only.) Wait a few minutes while the icing hardens, before moving on to assemble the train.

ASSEMBLING THE TRAIN

Since all the cars will be assembled on their sides, be gentle with the iced cookies to avoid cracking the hardened icing. Place the iced cookies on wax paper when assembling them. Clean the decorator and reload it with the white icing for construction of the cars.

Box Cars

Carefully place the box car pieces icing side down on the work surface. On one side piece, make a bead of icing along the three edges where the bottom and end pieces will sit. Also make a bead of icing on both ends of the bottom piece where it will join the end pieces. Stand the pieces in the beads of icing, making sure the bottom and ends meet. Hold or prop in place if necessary, until set. Construct each of the box cars in the same way.

When the pieces have hardened, make a bead of icing along the exposed edges. Set the other halves in place, lining the pieces up so the cars are square. Let the finished box cars harden while still on their sides, and then set them upright.

Coal Car

The coal car is assembled in exactly the same way as the box cars, so follow the box car instructions. When the coal car has set and can be placed in an upright position, ice the three exposed edges and carefully set the coal car roof in place.

Caboose

Again, the bottom portion of the caboose is assembled just like the box cars, so follow those instructions and you'll have your base. While the base is setting, construct the top compartment of the caboose.

Lay the four wall pieces on the work surface smooth side down. Make beads of icing along the vertical edges of the side walls and stand the ends in place. When the caboose base is in the upright position, make a bead of icing

Assemble the train engine on its side

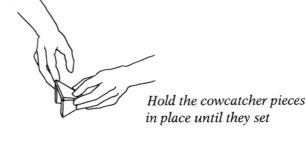

Hold the cowcatcher pieces in place until they set

Assemble the smokestack upside down, holding it until it has set

Attach the cowcatcher and hold in place

along the top exposed edges and set the large roof in place. Then make a bead of icing along the exposed edges of the upper compartment and set the iced edge on the caboose's large roof, making sure to center it.

Ice along the now-exposed edges of the upper compartment and set the small roof in place.

Engine

The train's engine is made in a similar fashion to the box cars and coal car. Place the side piece, icing facing down, on the table. Make a bead of icing along the edge where the back piece and bottom piece will be set. Also make a bead along the end of the bottom piece where it will meet the end piece. Stand the bottom and end pieces in place, propping if necessary. Relax a minute while these set, and begin construction of the cowcatcher and smokestack.

Cowcatcher

Place the four cowcatcher pieces on the table, smooth sides down. Make beads of icing along the edges of the two side pieces where they will attach to the bottom. Set them in place. Then make beads of icing along the two edges of the top piece and set it between the two side pieces. Hold these in place for a moment, until they set.

Smokestack

Lay the four smokestack pieces on the table with their smooth sides facing down. Make beads of icing along the right edge of each piece and assemble the four pieces, each overlapping the next, so as to keep the pieces square. Hold them in place while they set.

Now the train engine should be set, so make a bead of icing along the exposed edges and set the other half in place, lining up the sides. Leave this to set, and when it is thoroughly hardened, turn the engine upright and make a bead of icing along the exposed side edges. Set the two top pieces in place. Let the pieces set. Make a bead of icing along the base of the smokestack and place the smokestack on the engine, in the middle. Make a bead of icing around the front exposed edges and set the smokestack in place as well, propping if necessary.

Turn all the cars upright. Make thin beads of icing along the upper edges of the cars and set little disc candies into the icing.

Now it's time to assemble your train in its proper order. Place the locomotive at the front, the coal car behind it, the three box cars behind that, and let the caboose bring up the rear. Fill the box cars with your favorite goodies—candies, cookies, or even ice cream will make wonderful cargo. Now fire up the locomotive with chocolate nonpareils, and off you go!

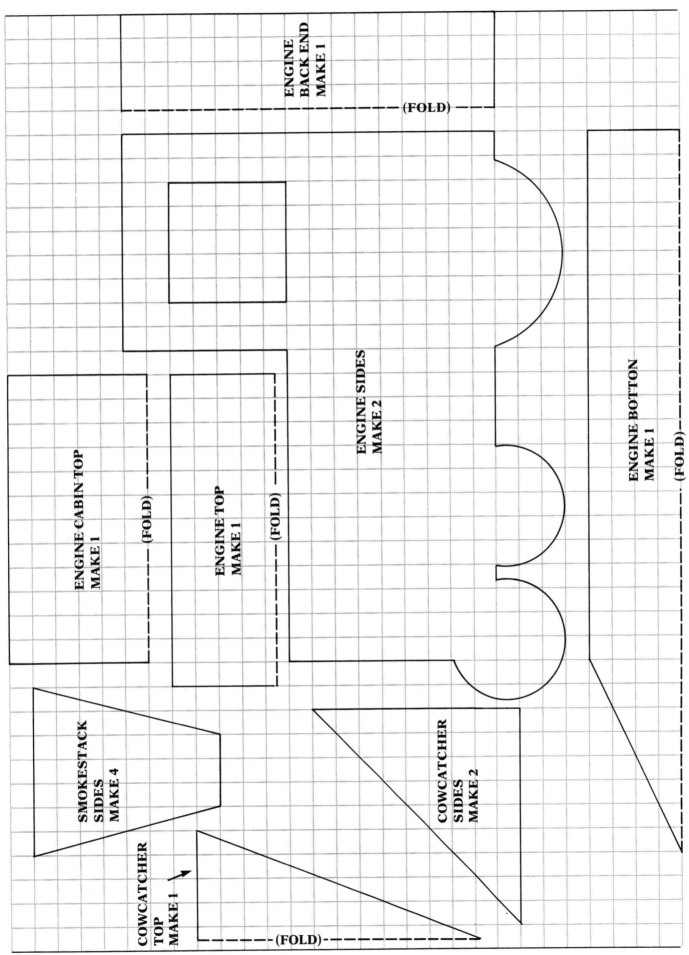

ENGINE BACK END
MAKE 1

(FOLD)

ENGINE CABIN TOP
MAKE 1

(FOLD)

ENGINE TOP
MAKE 1

(FOLD)

ENGINE SIDES
MAKE 2

ENGINE BOTTON
MAKE 1

(FOLD)

SMOKESTACK
SIDES
MAKE 4

COWCATCHER
TOP
MAKE 1

COWCATCHER
SIDES
MAKE 2

(FOLD)

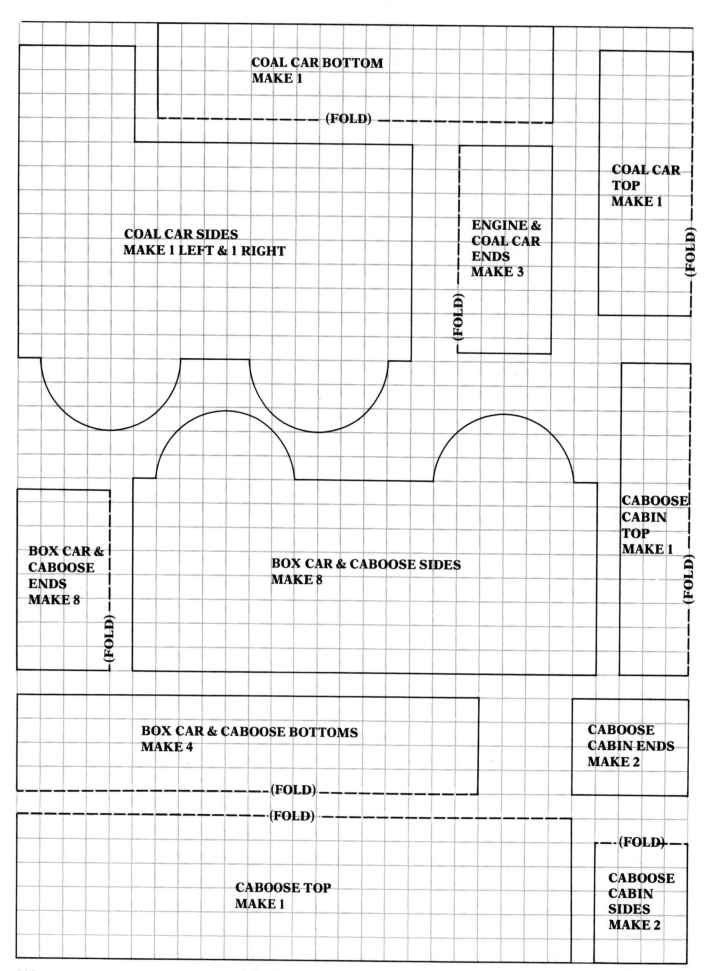

**COAL CAR BOTTOM
MAKE 1**

————————————— (FOLD) —————————————

**COAL CAR
TOP
MAKE 1**

**COAL CAR SIDES
MAKE 1 LEFT & 1 RIGHT**

**ENGINE &
COAL CAR
ENDS
MAKE 3**

(FOLD)

(FOLD)

**CABOOSE
CABIN
TOP
MAKE 1**

(FOLD)

**BOX CAR &
CABOOSE
ENDS
MAKE 8**

**BOX CAR & CABOOSE SIDES
MAKE 8**

(FOLD)

**BOX CAR & CABOOSE BOTTOMS
MAKE 4**

**CABOOSE
CABIN ENDS
MAKE 2**

————————————— (FOLD) —————————————

————————————— (FOLD) —————————————

————— (FOLD) —————

**CABOOSE TOP
MAKE 1**

**CABOOSE
CABIN
SIDES
MAKE 2**

14

SANTA AND SLED

egin a new family tradition this year by making this charming Christmas centerpiece. Santa and his sled full of goodies, pulled by the
eight famous reindeer, are sure to instill Christmas spirit in the heart of the
biggest Scrooge on your block. Helping to build it will keep your children's
minds off of where you hid the presents!

Have the following materials and ingredients handy before beginning
construction of Santa and his sled:

INGREDIENTS

Vanilla Cookie Dough: one batch
  (See p. 13.)
Icing: white for assembly (See p. 17.)
Red and green food color or paste
  for decorative icing

Chocolate kisses, multicolored
  mints, large raspberry drops or
  gumdrops, red hots or other
  favorite candies for added
  decoration

MATERIALS

Pattern pieces, cut out and
  labeled (See p. 10.)
Cookie cutters for extra cookies

Base, at least 14" x 18"
Cake decorator or pastry bag, and
  an assortment of tips

Mix and roll out your dough, cut out the paper pattern pieces and bake
the gingerbread parts according to the basic instructions found on pp. 10-
16. Once you've baked the gingerbread pieces and allowed them to cool
fully, you're ready to do some pre-assembly decoration. (Remember that
you should have four "left" and four "right" reindeer.)

For this project, it is a good idea to decorate the standing figures (Santa
and the reindeer) before assembling them.

DECORATING THE FIGURES

Separate the icing into one large batch and two small batches, in three
separate bowls. Set aside the large batch—covered, so it doesn't harden—to
be used for assembly, and carefully mix food paste into the other two bowls,
one red and one green. Add the food color a little at a time, until you reach
rich Christmas shades.

Fill the decorator with red icing and, using the small tip, pipe red beads
along the edges of Santa, his sled and the reindeer—remembering to decorate the smooth sides only. (These are the sides that will face out when you
assemble the pieces.) Add more red icing beads to Santa, delineating his
hat, belt, moustache and beard.

When you're done with any red decoration you desire, clean the decorator and fill it with green icing. Using the small tip, give Santa and his reindeer eyes. Adorn the sled and reindeer with wreaths and flowers, setting

individual red hots in the center of each. When all the cookie figures are iced to your liking, set them aside and move on to assembling the sled.

ASSEMBLING THE SLED

Constructing the sled is easily accomplished when it is on its side. First, place one with the icing side down on waxed paper. Apply beads of icing where the back, front, center and floor pieces will connect with it. Then ice the edges of the short ends of the back and front pieces, and join them to the side piece. Hold or prop until the icing hardens. Then ice the sides of the front and back pieces, and join them to the side piece, propping or holding them in place until all the icing joints are secure.

Make beads of icing along the exposed edges of the back, middle and bottom pieces, and carefully set the remaining side piece of the sled into place. Allow ample time for hardening before standing it upright. Now that the sled is done, you'll need to hitch up the trusty reindeer to pull it.

ASSEMBLING THE REINDEER

Like the sled, assemble the reindeer on their sides. Carefully, to avoid cracking the icing decoration, lay one reindeer icing side down on waxed paper. Squeeze beads of icing along the outer edges of the two spreaders, and place them on the reindeer. Repeat with the three other reindeer that face the same direction. Be careful not to damage the icing you added earlier. You should now have four reindeer attached to spreaders, waiting for their four counterparts on the other side.

Go wrap a present, or put another log on the fire. . . . You want to give the icing time to dry.

When the spreaders are firmly set, put beads of icing along their exposed edges and attach the other reindeer, icing side up. Let them set thoroughly before standing them on their "hooves."

Set the reindeer up in front of the sled, and secure both reindeer and sled to the base with small dabs of icing. From Santa and his sled to the line of reindeer, carefully drape thin strings of red licorice for the reins, tacking them with dots of icing. Using dabs oficing for glue, place large raspberry drops along the border of the base. Scatter large colored mints on the base to create snow-covered ground, and you're just about done. All you have to do is place Santa firmly on his sled with a bead of icing, and he's ready to take off on his once-a-year, special-delivery mission.

Add beads of icing where the back, front, center and floor pieces will be attached

Set the second side of the sled in place

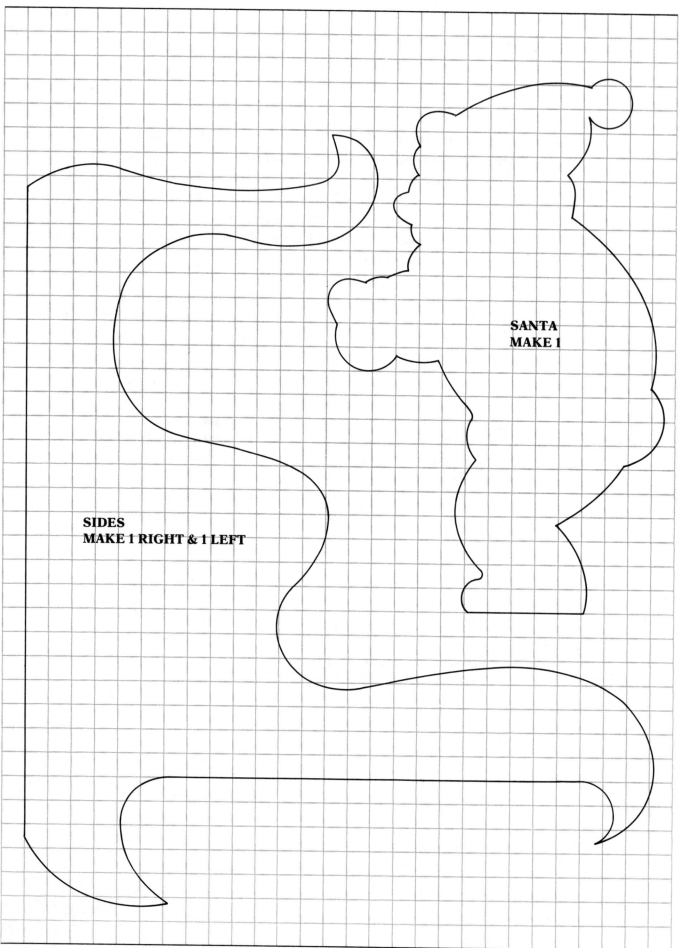

SANTA
MAKE 1

SIDES
MAKE 1 RIGHT & 1 LEFT

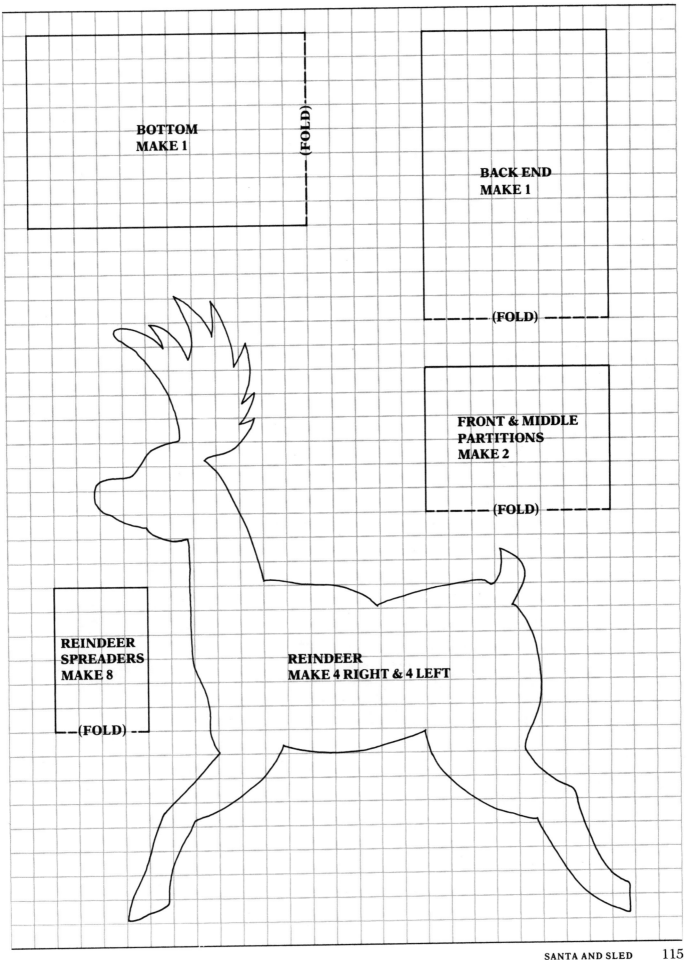

BOTTOM
MAKE 1

(FOLD)

BACK END
MAKE 1

(FOLD)

FRONT & MIDDLE
PARTITIONS
MAKE 2

(FOLD)

REINDEER
SPREADERS
MAKE 8

(FOLD)

REINDEER
MAKE 4 RIGHT & 4 LEFT

15

·•·•·•·•·•·•·•·•·•·•·

CRECHE

The Christmas season is the ideal—and traditional—time to undertake a gingerbread project. You're bound to have plenty of helpers home on Christmas vacation, and lots of guests dropping by to admire your handiwork. This gingerbread Nativity scene is a lovely way to mark the season, and building it may even become an annual family event.

The biblical scene features the three wise men and their camels, the shepherd boy and his flock, the holy family, and of course the shining star of Bethlehem.

Before beginning to build the Crèche, have the following ingredients and materials handy:

INGREDIENTS

Vanilla Cookie Dough: one batch
   (See p. 13.)
Icing: white for assembly (See p. 17.)
Yellow and green food color or
   paste

Glaze (See p. 20.)
Oatmeal
Raspberry drops
Red hots
Chocolate kisses

MATERIALS

Pattern pieces, cut out and labeled
   (See p. 10-16.)
Cake decorator or pastry bag
Base, at least 14″ x 18″

Brush for glaze
1 toothpick
String

Mix and roll out your dough, cut out the paper pattern pieces and bake the gingerbread parts according to the basic instructions found on pp. 10-16. While your star cookie is still soft, gently insert one end of the toothpick, and set it aside for later.

After you've baked and cooled all of the Crèche parts, and the people and animal cookies as well, you are ready to begin construction.

CRECHE ASSEMBLY

The building itself is a simple shed, open on one side and very easy to build. Since the front is open and the inside is exposed, make sure that the good sides of the back, side and bottom pieces are facing front and inside.

Place the back, side and bottom pieces smooth side up on the table, side by side. Make beads of icing along the vertical wall joints. Stand up the back piece and one side piece against the edge of the bottom piece. Then, add the other side piece in the same way. Prop up the structure if necessary, and tie with lengths of string until they are set. (Tying a three-sided structure can be tricky; don't tie it too tightly.) You can add a temporary cardboard piece for the front wall to make tying easier.

*Assemble the manger
on its side*

*Stand the figures into mounds
of half-hardened icing*

Make a bead of icing along the base to secure the walls, and allow the whole thing to set for about 10 minutes. When it is firm, add the roof.

Roof

Place the two roof sections smooth side up, side by side on the table with 1/8" space between them. Make a bead of icing along the space and push the pieces together to form a joint. Make a bead of icing along the top edges of the side walls and the gable of the back piece. Place the roof pieces carefully in position on the walls and hold for a moment, until they begin to set. Tie lengths of string around the roof—front and back—and prop up the front if necessary. Allow the roof to set for 10 minutes or so, and then go on to assemble the manger.

Manger

Place the side pieces, end pieces and bottom of the manger smooth side down. Make beads of icing along the edges where the pieces will join. Raise the four sides and hold or prop them until the icing has hardened.

Your Crèche is all built, and ready to be decorated and populated.

DECORATING THE CRECHE

Divide your remaining icing in half, in two small bowls. Mix in food color or paste, making one batch of green and one batch of golden yellow icing.

Using a thin, plain tip on your pastry bag or cake decorator, add yellow decoration to your star cookie. Carefully stick it into the roof peak with the toothpick, and secure with a bit of icing. Using a fine tip, give the camels, sheep, cows and donkey yellow eyes and outlines. Then add yellow decoration to the wisemen, shepherd boy and holy family. Allow the icing to set. To stand the cookies up in position on your base, make mounds of icing where you will place them. While waiting for these mounds to harden just a little, plan where the people and animals will go. The shepherd and sheep, the wisemen and camels, and the holy family should be placed around the manger. The cows and donkey can be in the background, looking on.

When the icing mounds have had a chance to set a bit, stand the cookies up in the icing, propping if necessary.

Clean your decorator and fill it with the green icing. Using a fluted tip, make a bead of icing along the peak and edges of the roof and along the base of the shed. Make a bead of icing along the outside edges of the base. Place raspberry drops in the icing, forming a border.

Brush the glaze on the roof and ground area (anywhere where the base is still exposed). Sprinkle the roof and ground liberally with oatmeal. Scatter a few red hots for color. Place some chocolate kisses at the feet of the wisemen, to represent their bountiful gifts.

Your sacred scene is complete, the elegant gold figures standing out against the simple, pastoral structure. Your Crèche will stay fresh and festive throughout the holiday season—you might even want to place it in a window on Christmas Eve.

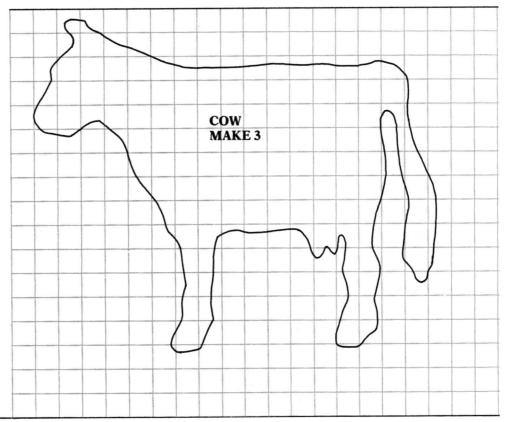

COW
MAKE 3

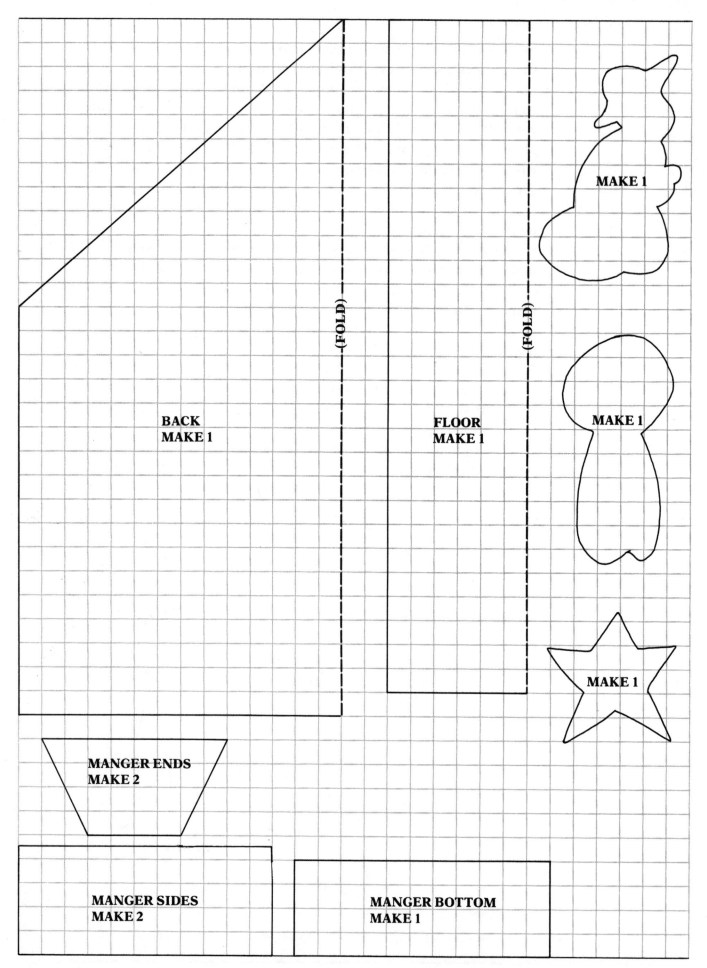

BACK
MAKE 1

FLOOR
MAKE 1

(FOLD)

(FOLD)

MAKE 1

MAKE 1

MAKE 1

MANGER ENDS
MAKE 2

MANGER SIDES
MAKE 2

MANGER BOTTOM
MAKE 1

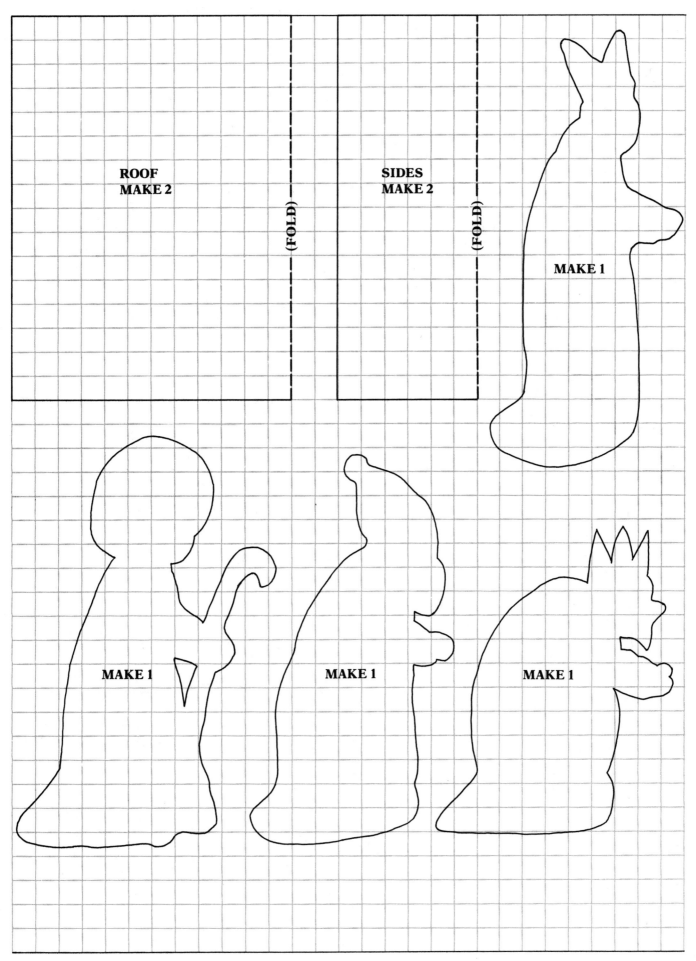

ROOF
MAKE 2

(FOLD)

SIDES
MAKE 2

(FOLD)

MAKE 1

MAKE 1

MAKE 1

MAKE 1

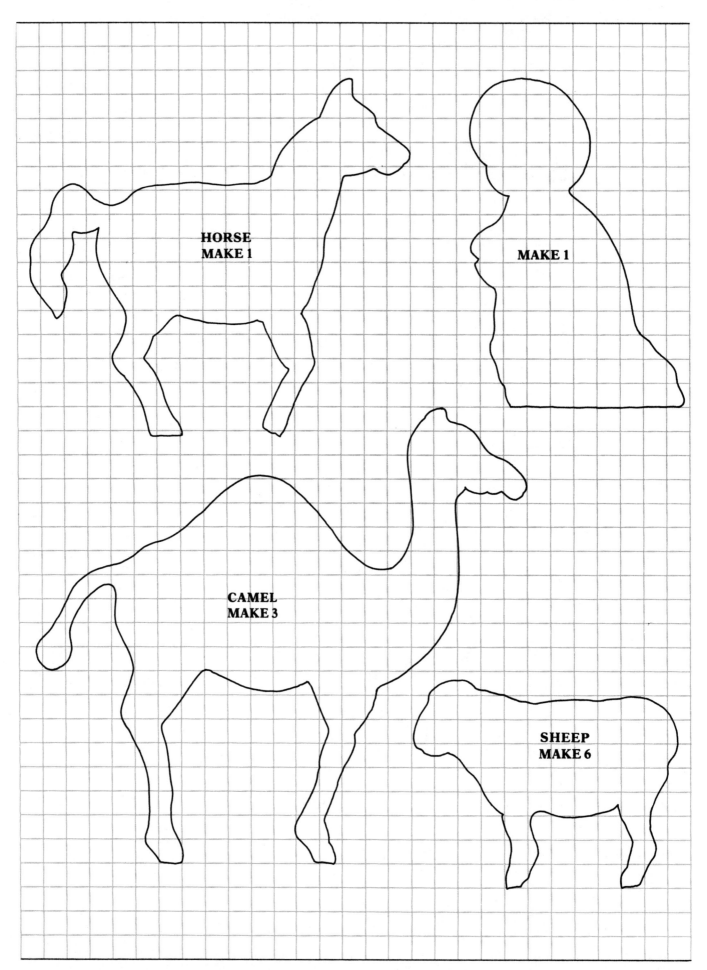

HORSE
MAKE 1

MAKE 1

CAMEL
MAKE 3

SHEEP
MAKE 6

16

● ● ● ● ● ● ● ● ● ● ● ● ● ● ● ● ● ●

MORE COOKIES

Decorated cookies are an essential part of making gingerbread houses. They serve as snacks for your workers and props to complete the theme of the house or other project. The following patterns are only suggestions—you can draw and cut patterns for anything you dream up, so use your imagination.

Remember to fit the cookie patterns carefully onto the rolled-out dough, to make the best possible use of space.

After the cookies have been baked and cooled, you can decorate them with beads and dots of colored icing and small bits of candy, giving them features, clothing and personality. Stand them up in mounds of partially set icing around your house after it's complete. Groups of figures or animals are more effective than single cookies. Remember that some are bound to get snitched while you're not looking—you might even be tempted yourself—so make lots to share and enjoy.

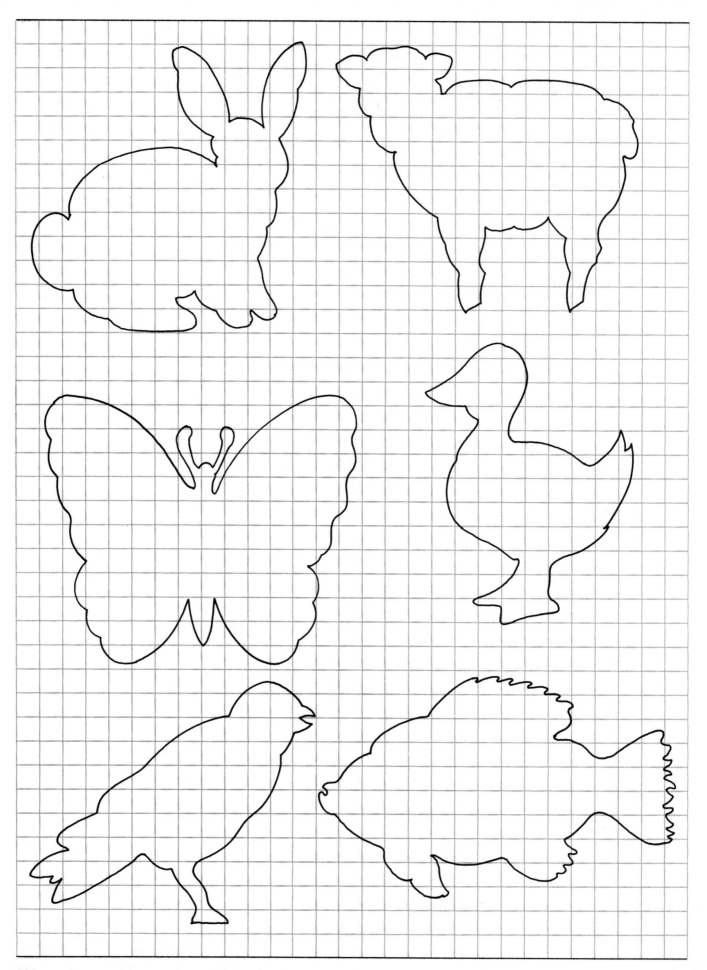

Happy Birthday

ABOUT THE AUTHORS

Lauren Jarrett is a watercolorist of childhood, domestic and nature themes who lives in East Hampton, New York. She illustrates cookbooks, gardening books and nature books when not working for The Nature Conservancy or feeding friends in East Hampton or Denver.

Nancy Nagle enjoys the arts of cooking, flower and vegetable gardening and photography. She lives with her husband Bill, an artist, in East Hampton, New York.